AWAKEN

THE

SPIRIT

WITHIN

AWAKEN
THE
SPIRIT
WITHIN

◄O►

10 Steps to Ignite Your Life

and Fulfill Your Divine Purpose

◄O►

Rebecca Rosen

WITH Samantha Rose

HARMONY

BOOKS • NEW YORK

Published in the United States by Harmony Books, an imprint
of the Crown Publishing Group, a division of Random House,
Inc., New York.
www.crownpublishing.com

Harmony Books is a registered trademark of Random House,
Inc., and the Circle colophon is a trademark of Random
House, Inc.

Library of Congress Cataloging-in-Publication Data
Rosen, Rebecca, 1976-
Awaken the spirit within: 10 ways to ignite your life and fulfill
your divine purpose / by Rebecca Rosen with Samantha Rose.—
First edition.
1. Health—Popular works. 2. Mind and body—Popular works.
3. Spirituality—Popular works. I. Rose, Samantha. II. Title.
RA776.9.R67 2013
613—dc23   2013000618

ISBN 978-0-7704-3751-0
eISBN 978-0-7704-3752-7

Printed in the United States of America

Illustration by Fred Haynes
Jacket design by Nupoor Gordon
Jacket photograph by Brett Seeley

10 9 8 7 6 5 4 3 2 1

First Edition

To my little light sparks, Jakob and Sam.

Your growth provides a constant source of joy, pride,

and inspiration. You fill my heart with

immeasurable love, reminding me of who I am

and why I am here.

Contents

━◀◉▶━

Introduction: ARE YOU AWAKE?

Lately, everywhere I go—the gym, the grocery store, my neighborhood Starbucks—I notice people who look like they're sleepwalking through life. Distracted, disconnected, I see them stumbling around, going through their everyday motions, but not fully *awake* to their lives. At the office, I've also noticed a general fogginess reflected in many of my clients. Both women and men of all ages, from kindergarten teachers to CEOs, show up at my doorstep lost and confused, like they haven't yet had their first cup of morning coffee. They plead with me to give them clarity. They want to know, "Where is my life going? Why do I feel like I'm running in circles?" Some show up searching for deeper understanding. They want to know, "Rebecca, can I ever truly be happy and fulfilled in life?" Some boldly ask, "What's the *point* of my life? Help me understand what I'm meant to do." They're desperate for answers, and they look to me to give them clear direction.

Well, if you read my first book, *Spirited,* or if you've seen me explaining my unconventional profession on TV or in magazine articles, you know that I'm not a shrink, a hypnotherapist, or a life coach, but a spiritual medium. I make my living communicating with those who are no longer living, and who have important insights for those who still are. That's right—I talk to the dead. I like to refer to myself as a middle gal between this world and the next, and what I hear time and time again from spiritual beings who've "crossed over" is the same simple yet urgent plea: *Wake up before it's too late!*

Now, I don't say this to spook or scare you, but to jump-start your enthusiasm and fire up your own desire to wake up, to become completely engaged in your life and excited about where it's going. That you've been guided, either consciously or unconsciously, to pick up this book means you, too, are craving some degree of clarity, resolve, and direction in your own life. So consider what I'm about to share with you in the pages ahead your official wake-up call.

Over the years, in addition to consoling thousands of clients who are grieving the loss of a cherished loved one, I've used my heightened sensitivity and intuitive and spiritual gifts to help just as many people overcome everyday obstacles standing in their way—be it a weight struggle, financial hardship, job dissatisfaction, or a relationship hiccup—so they can move forward with their lives. In fact, the inspiration to write *Spirited* came after countless hours of spiritual readings turned counseling sessions, where the dead came through with very down-to-Earth advice for solving real-life problems. I realized then that if I provided my clients with the same spiritual tools and intuitive insight that I use every day, they could learn to move past life's roadblocks all on their own.

Now, in *Awaken the Spirit Within,* it's my intention to further empower you by revealing not only where on the road of life you are, but also where that road is *ultimately taking you.* In other words—I want to help you identify the very point of your life. Big stuff, yes, and imagine how gaining this level of clarity might change not only your current outlook on life, but also your overall mood, your relationships, and your day-to-day routine. Imagine how you might feel if tomorrow morning you woke up absolutely clear and confidant about *who you're meant to be and what you're meant to do.* Can you imagine the kind of relief that comes with knowing where your life is headed beyond the nine-to-five grind? To find out, keep reading.

After communicating for almost fifteen years now with enlightened spiritual beings who have given me unquestionably real validation that I'm indeed connecting with the other side, what I understand and know on a deep soul level is that there *is* a point to each of our lives. Every one of us has been put on this Earth, at this exact moment in time, with a very intentional direction, along with sight markers and a road map to help get us there. That said, many of us have lost our way. We've driven off the rails, ignored signs of caution, hit major roadblocks, and in some cases, we've completely fallen asleep at the wheel. Getting back on track is what many refer to as *living your life on purpose.* I call it being awake, and in my world of the weird I do this by connecting with something deep within myself and also with a spiritual support system much bigger than me to help guide me along—and that's what this book will teach you to do.

In our hearts, most of us yearn to feel connected to something bigger, don't we? A bigger goal, a clearer mission, a higher purpose. And while a lot of books have been written about the importance and reward of living a life "on purpose," what's different about my message is the unconventional (okay, a little oddball) sources I use to support it. My insights come from deceased loved ones, spirit guides, angelic and spiritually enlightened beings of light whose sole intention is to help us learn and grow throughout our lifetime on Earth. I refer to this collective guidance as "Spirit," and what it confirms for me on a daily basis is that how you approach and live your life absolutely matters. The choices you make daily either position you in a direction toward happiness and fulfillment or they lead you astray. Sadly, many of us, and often unconsciously, choose the latter, and it only takes a few wrong turns before you're driving down a very dark and lonely highway. Perhaps you've found yourself stuck out in the middle of nowhere? Not to worry. You will learn how to change course *right now.*

At any given moment, everyone you know is at a different point on the road of life. You very well may be someone who's essentially on track, with a need only for minor adjustments. Or you may be someone who's hit a dead end; you need to make a complete U-turn. Wherever you are, in the pages ahead I will share with you a set of ten powerful yet simple steps to guide you forward. These ten steps of awakening are based on the ancient mystical wisdom of the Kabbalah that seeks to answer why we exist, why we're born, where we come from, and where we're going in our lives. Inspired by both my study of the Kabbalah and my own personal experiences and unique perspective as a professional spiritual medium, you'll soon discover that every day provides you with new opportunities to reignite your life and move forward toward fulfilling your life's intended and divine purpose.

For many, the idea that the unseen world can be a source of clarity and guidance in our earthly lives sounds illogical and even ridiculous, and if you also find yourself scratching your head, take a minute and consider this— who better to shed light on our lives than those who've already lived, and who share a special bond with us based on our similar life experiences? Take it from someone who converses with the other side on a day-to-day basis: Enlightened spiritual beings have valuable and insightful lessons to share. They *know* things, they've *seen* things, and they have a far greater perspective than we can even imagine! Where we only see the fog from the ground, they see the sun behind the clouds. And believe it or not, spiritual guidance as I'm describing it is not just reserved for woo-woos like me. We *all* have this guidance available to us, to turn to when we need it. And when you think about it—doesn't that make sense? Humans have never been solitary beings. Why should we have to face life's biggest challenges by going it alone? If exploring the unseen world makes you a little bit squirmy, let me assure you—there's nothing dark or scary in what I do. I work exclusively with loving energy and light, and that's exactly what I'll teach you to do.

Not sure you believe it? Does this sound like hocus-pocus?

If so, then consider that I've accurately served as a bridge between this world and the next for thousands of clients for more than a decade, and I currently have a three-year waiting list of new and returning clients. I've turned even more skeptics into believers, and not because I've mastered the ultimate party trick (channeling the dead ranks pretty high up on the list) but because the work speaks for itself. Meaning, *Spirit speaks for itself.* I'm just a messenger. In fact, I believe it's my professional obligation and responsibility to take myself out of the conversation entirely. My role is not to question or judge but to simply serve as an open, neutral conduit for information to pass through.

When I clear my head of any and all personal thoughts, feelings, or opinions, I'm able to deliver detailed, meaningful, and accurate messages from the spirit world to my clients. I really cannot tell you how often the spiritual insights I deliver in both private readings and group seminars elicit looks of utter shock. I've seen jaws drop open, furrowed brows of disbelief. "How could you *know* that?" is a reaction I get all the time.

The answer is that I know what I know by relying on a combination of intuitive tools and mental impressions called *clairs* that flood my mind when I'm in a heightened energetic state (more on this later, but for now let me assure you this doesn't involve speaking in tongues or rolling my eyes backward into my head!). When I'm in this higher state of mind, Spirit uses clairsentience (clear feelings), clairvoyance (clear seeing), clairaudience (clear hearing), and claircognizance (plain-as-day clear knowing) to deliver information and messages from the unseen world and higher spiritual realms, which I then pass on to clients—things that only the person I'm reading could know—and this information works as proof and validation that spirit communication is indeed taking place.

For example, on a phone call with a female client that for the purposes of privacy I'll call "Rosie," I received insights from her deceased maternal grandmother. (Most of my private readings are delivered over the phone. To understand how this works, know that spirits aren't limited to space and time like we are. Where we only wish we could be in more than one place at one time, spirits can be anywhere and everywhere—one of the perks of the afterlife. If I'm in Denver and my client is in San Francisco, it doesn't matter; Spirit can be present with both of us.) Rosie's grandma in spirit clairvoyantly impressed upon my mind a green stone, so I asked Rosie, "What's the significance of the green stone? Do you have a piece of jewelry with a green stone that holds special meaning?" There was silence on the other end of the line followed by a shaky whisper, "No way." Sure enough, my client had, moments before our call, put on a jade necklace that Grandma had given to her when she was still alive.

In another phone reading, I picked up on the spunky energy of a woman who kept nudging me to ask her living daughter about her shoes. So I asked my client, "Are you wearing your mom's shoes?" I thought maybe Mom was clairvoyantly impressing the image of a shoe in my mind to communicate that, metaphorically, her daughter had stepped up, stepped into her shoes. But actually, Mom was being quite literal, because what my client confirmed was that after her mom's death, she'd kept all of her shoes, including many they'd shopped for together, as sentimental keepsakes; and because they were the same size, she'd slipped a pair of them on moments before our reading. She really *was* wearing her mom's shoes.

These might seem like silly and trivial details. You may be asking yourself, "What do spirits care about what we're wearing?" The answer is: They don't care. But they will use specific details like this to provide undeniable proof to their living loved ones that their spirits are eternal and they're still a continued presence in their lives. At this magic moment, when clients understand that there really is life after death, I can almost hear an energetic shift in their voices. If I'm doing a face-to-face reading, I will often see visible changes in the client's face and body, like a heavy weight has been lifted off of the client. When they realize they aren't alone and that love surrounds them, clients regularly break down in tears. They understand and *feel* on a deep level that I've connected them to a cherished loved one who is no longer walking on this Earth but is still very alive and present in their lives. This is often all they've been longing to hear in order to move past their grief and step forward with their lives.

I don't share these stories to impress you or score bragging rights in my psychic social circles. Truly, I'm humbled by what I'm able to do, and often I'm in awe myself. I regard my ability to connect with Spirit as a gift and a tremendous source of healing. It's my honor to provide comfort and peace to those who desperately need closure after the loss of a loved one, and also to those who seek general guidance and clarity in their day-to-day lives. It brings me great joy to be able to share my gift and my knowing with you today.

My intention is for you to come to know what Spirit communicates to me over and over and over again—there's a purpose for your life that was scripted before you were born. That's right, you came into this world knowing exactly what you're meant to do—but you may have forgotten what that is. You've fallen asleep. And now you're about to wake up.

Granted, waking up to your life's purpose might sound like an elusive goal and a downright luxury if you're struggling to pay the mortgage, overcome a health issue, or save a crumbling marriage, but the truth is that when you come to understand the bigger picture, you'll gain a focused understanding of why your present day reality looks *exactly the way it does*—why events, people, and circumstances have shown up in your life just the way they have. And with this new clarity and awareness, your day-to-day life will not only take on greater and deeper meaning, but also likely begin to change in very real, tangible ways. For example, you may experience the following shifts in your waking life:

- More peace and fulfillment in your personal relationships
- Confidence in your natural talents and abilities
- Greater opportunities and success on the job

- Financial abundance and prosperity
- The courage to conquer addictions
- Freedom from weight struggles and poor body image
- The clarity to make the "right" choices and decisions for your life
- An everyday outlook that's not fear or anxiety based, but instead happy, hopeful, and joyful

As you can see, when you follow the ten steps in *Awaken the Spirit Within*, many of your daily struggles—both the heavy burdens and the small irritations—will start to lift. No kidding, you may actually begin to *feel* lighter. And with this lightness, your life will begin to flow in the direction it's intended to go. Now, I can't promise you that your life will be perfect. I wouldn't place any bets on winning the lottery tonight or losing ten pounds by tomorrow morning. Roadblocks and setbacks are an inevitable part of the life journey, but what you'll also come to learn is that every bump in the road is an opportunity to regain your focus, make adjustments, and get back on track.

So what do you say?

Are you up for the ride?

Then buckle up. Your life is about to take off and expand in ways you never thought possible. To borrow from one of my favorite romantic comedies, *Joe Versus the Volcano*, "Almost the whole world is asleep. Everybody you know. Everybody you see. Everybody you talk to . . . only a few people are awake and they live in a state of constant total amazement."

PART ONE

YOUR PURPOSE

Lᴇᴛ's ɢᴇᴛ ʀɪɢʜᴛ ᴛᴏ ɪᴛ—ᴛᴏ fulfill your purpose in life all you need to do is just be yourself and start shining.

Really.

If you think that's just a load of New Age hooey, well then consider this—maybe you don't know *who* or *what* you really are. The truth is, most of us don't know what we're made of. So let's start there.

In my first book, *Spirited*, I explained to readers that you fulfill your life's purpose by being the highest expression of yourself, and when your actions, words, and thoughts are kind, gentle, gracious, and loving, you're doing just *that*. While I still maintain and know this to be true, further clarification may be in order. Allow me: When your actions, words, and thoughts are kind, gentle, gracious, and loving, you're expressing your divinity, your God-spark within, and *that* is your purpose in life. Yes, we're only a few pages in and I've already dropped G-O-D into the conversation.

Let me explain what God means to me, and before I do I want to be very clear on two points. First, God is just the word I use to identify something that you may have another perfectly good word for—Source, Higher Power, Creator, and the Universe are popular alternates. And secondly, it's not my intention to challenge or validate your particular belief system, but only to share the messages and insight that Spirit has passed on to me. Remember, I'm just the messenger.

For the fifteen years that I've served as a medium between this world and the next, what Spirit has clairvoyantly, clairsentiently, clairaudiently, and claircognizantly impressed upon me is that God is pure, unconditional loving energy. What I've personally experienced, believe, and now know to be true is that God is the highest vibrational energy that exists in the universe. God is the source of all energy. And since everything that you can think of is made up of energy that never dies but simply changes form, then I bet you can see where I'm headed here—you and me, each and every one of us on Earth, are, in our simplest form, energetic extensions of God. In other words: a chip off the old block.

What spirits, those who have died a physical death on Earth and crossed over to the higher, brighter spiritual realms, confirm for me on a daily basis is that we are each living, walking, talking, and breathing manifestations of God. We're all packaged differently, but our insides—our spirits—are made of the same stuff: divine loving energy and light. I like to think of it this way—within each of us is God's incredible and powerful DNA. Meaning you have all the qualities, all the wonderful, radiant expressions of God, already inside you.

Say what? God's DNA—really, I'm not making this up. According to Kabbalah, the mystical branch of Judaism, ten powerful expressions, or characteristics, of God reside within, permeate, and surround each and every one of us. I'm talking about things like compassion, kindness, trust, and gratitude. Buddhists call this the "Germ of Buddhahood," or the "Buddha-nature." Hinduism calls this the "Atman" and Christians call this the "Holy Spirit." However and whatever you want to call it, the principle is the same: When you express your innate divinity, God is revealed through you, as you. Kabbalists refer to this as "letting in the light," where all ten expressions of God are awakened, lit, or *ignited* and man ascends the mystical Tree of Life.

AN ENERGETIC EXTENSION OF GOD

In your simplest form, you are pure and powerful energy and light. This energy that flows within you is called by many names. In ancient Chinese medicine, it's called Chi. In yoga, it's called Shakti. In the West, it's commonly called Spirit. I often refer to it as our God-spark. All great spiritual traditions talk about spiritual energy and the energetic body; they just give them different names. Whatever the tradition, the assertion is the same—the energy and light within and throughout you is meant to *flow*. This is what it means to awaken the spirit within.

Throughout the pages of this book, I'll reference the principles of many different belief systems, but I want to be clear—my definition of God has no ties to any religious affiliation. Rather, what I know to be true comes from countless insights backed by clear validations from Spirit. What Spirit has communicated to me time and time again is that there are no denominations (Christian, Buddhist, Jewish, Islam, etc.) on the other side. When all is said and done, *and by done I mean dead,* we all end up in the same place despite our personal beliefs or philosophies in life. I call this place, this sacred space, God. I also call it home.

If you doubt, distrust, or even outright reject an all-inclusive ideology, you're not alone. In readings, spirits often share with me their stunned realization that their path to God in life was not *the* way, but only *a* way and that truly, all paths lead home. Consider that God, metaphorically, is the center of a wheel. The spokes on the wheel represent the many unique and different paths people use to reach God, and yet each spoke is connected to the same central hub. Meaning that all religions, all paths serve a similar purpose—to connect us to and bring us closer to God. In fact, the root of the word *religion* means "to bind" or "to connect." When you think about it, whether you practice Catholicism, Judaism, Buddhism, any other religion, or Atheism, it's really meaningful and purposeful connection that you're after, isn't it? So you see, no matter what your religion or belief system, we're all searching for and wanting the same basic stuff.

As a general rule, I try to leave theological discussions out of my work because religion has a tendency to polarize people. And yet it comes up anyway, and not from my living clients, but from the dead! What I hear nearly every day in readings with Spirit is how their faith in something bigger and beyond helped ease the deceased's transition from life into death. In most cases, death looks, feels, and *is* different than what the deceased imagined it would be, but if they already believed in something in life, they readily embrace and transition into the afterlife, no problem, no question. Conversely, many spirits who died without having faith in God or something more acknowledge a complete turnaround in their belief system in death. Where in life they were plagued by doubt or skepticism, in death they clairsentiently express a feeling of overwhelming love and understanding of our divine oneness and that—spoiler alert—we don't have to wait until our physical body dies to know and feel God.

BELIEF IN SOMETHING MORE

Jennifer's Story

"I have a young man; is he your son?" Rebecca said to my mother. Then she turned to me and said, "I'm getting the sense he's your brother. He's front and center and coming through really strong." Those were the first words Rebecca said to us in our first reading with her, in March 2007, and what welcome words they were after nearly five years of grief and unanswered questions.

My brother Jeff died suddenly, unexpectedly, and tragically at age thirty-four. His death and its aftermath had left us hoping and searching for a reputable psychic medium for years. When we finally met Rebecca, we were unsure what to really expect. We didn't fully comprehend the enormity of it at the time, even after it was over, but that day changed our lives and understanding of life and death forever.

After Jeff's death, we turned to God and churches for answers. But at the same time, we struggled to truly believe in a God that would allow such a tragedy to take place. We struggled not just because this tragedy happened in our family, but also because many happen around the world every day to people of all ages and stations in life. When Jeff told us through Rebecca that we needed to put our trust in God, we were somewhat stunned and confused, since he had gone to church in life but was not a fervently religious person. He said we needed to be reminded of that frequently and that the best way to do so was to look at U.S. coins for a simple reminder— "In God We Trust,"—and that he would send them often as "signs" that he is around us. Moreover, he admitted that when he died, he didn't really believe in God or an afterlife. Now he knew differently.

This message from the spirit world may sound small, but it was a huge leap for us and our understanding of what lies beyond this earthly life. It took time for us to turn our thinking around this way, but five years beyond that day we don't question the existence of God anymore or life after this life. Our understanding of life and death has been altered irrevocably, leading to an awareness of spiritual matters that we never thought possible. We went from a place of deep grief, pain, and fear to a place of greater love.

In a reading with a young woman, her father in spirit identified himself to me and clairvoyantly showed me a rosary and a Buddha, while clairsentiently impressing me with an overwhelming feeling of unity, peace, connection, and oneness. I said to my client, "Was your dad a Catholic? Is there something going on in your life right now with conflicting religions, because Dad is telling me that where he is now—it's all one." My client gasped, and then told me that her father, who'd been a devout Catholic, had died not long after she'd gotten engaged to a Buddhist. He'd struggled with accepting his daughter's interfaith marriage. I said, "Well, he's saying that none of that matters now. He wants you to know he blesses the marriage."

I know I'm not breaking any big ground here. The idea that we're all connected and created in God's image is nothing new. Look no further than Genesis 1:27 in the Old Testament for one of the more celebrated references. And anyway, the popular Teilhard de Chardin adage that "we're all spiritual beings having a human experience," and not the other way around, might be something you've believed all along, or at least entertained as possibly true. But let me ask you this—what if you *knew* it to be true? What would it be like to *feel*, to experience this knowing way down, deep inside? Would it change how you felt about yourself and your life? Would it change how you felt about other people?

Before you think on this too long, let me go ahead and answer the question for you: The knowledge that you are an energetic extension of God's powerful energy, love, and light has the potential to change everything about

FINDING COMFORT IN ONENESS

The knowledge that we are each an energetic extension and expression of God, the most powerful energy force in the universe, is something I regularly share with my clients. To be expected, reactions to this news are mixed. Some embrace it with enthusiasm, while others express disappointment at the suggestion that God isn't something supreme and separate, ruling from above. One client expressed her vulnerability this way: "Believing in an all-powerful something that's outside of me that I can depend on and pray to gives me great comfort on days when I don't feel all that powerful on my own."

If you're feeling this way, too, take a moment and liken God to a magnificent and powerful fire, burning bright and with radiant intensity. Now consider that you were born from this fire, so within you burns a similar flame, only on a scale much smaller and not quite as bright. A God-spark, if you will.

The very purpose of awakening is to grow your divine radiance. As your fire begins to grow bigger and brighter, your connection to God's fiery intensity grows with it. In this respect, God is both outside of and within you. Get it?

your life because knowing this truth about yourself and then acting on it *is your purpose in life*.

Yes. It's that simple.

What Spirit has conveyed to me for more than a decade now is that our purpose, that elusive thing that all commencement speeches hint at but don't explain, is to show up every day and express and extend our divine radiance to the people and world around us. The question is: How?

By simply being *you*.

Easier said than done. And can you guess why?

MIND CONTROL

I receive valuable information, truths, and insights from enlightened spiritual beings not only through my heightened sensitivity and clairs, but also via my daily meditations and dreams. Meditation works like magic to lighten and heighten my energy, allowing me to move past the boundaries of this world and tap into the higher energies of the spirit world. Dreams can work in a similar way. Did you know that when we're dreaming our spirits regularly leave our physical bodies and travel to the other side, where we meet up with other people who are similarly dreaming? This is called astral travel and it may sound crazy, but I've experienced it enough times now to know it's true. It's not unusual for me to wake up in the morning with a very clear knowing of something I learned while my spirit was out cruising around. Often, I'm left with an unshakable image or feeling that provides insight into a situation I've been struggling with in my daily life or answers a question I've been wrestling around with in my head. Perhaps you've experienced the same sort of clarity after a good night's sleep?

In a recurring dream I've had for years, I'm hurrying down a Jetway toward a departing plane. I'm wearing a backpack that contains everything I need for my trip, and

I'm anxious to get on the plane and take my seat, except when I get to the end of the Jetway, there's no plane. Instead, I fall in line behind a number of people waiting to take their turn jumping down a big slide. This is not the emergency slide like you see illustrated in the airplane evacuation manual. This slide is more like a gigantic waterslide, like what you'd find at an amusement park, and it descends into brilliant, almost blinding white light. When I see this slide, I'm suddenly filled with excitement and joy, and I can hardly wait to take my turn. When I get to the front of the line, I take one deep breath and jump down the chute. When I enter the light, my spirit slips into my physical body and I am born.

As babies, we are energetic bundles of divine love and light—pure vessels containing God's powerful DNA—and yet almost as soon as we're born into this physical world, we begin to forget what we're truly made of and where we came from. We fall asleep. Or rather, our spirit nods off and our mind takes control of the wheel.

Ninety percent of the world lives in a mind existence; most of us are stuck in our heads. Given those numbers, odds are that you, too, are thinking your way through life. If you've fallen into the habit of listening to and being guided by your mind rather than your spirit, don't beat yourself up; the majority of us do it. It's hard, if not impossible, to avoid. The culture we live in is driven by our collective mind noise, which is extremely loud, persistent, and persuasive. Just try arguing with it! For sure, the mind can be a first-rate know-it-all. An antagonizer. And most of us can only take so much of getting pushed around and *beaten down* before we grow weak and weary.

GET HIGHER, BABY

In my line of work, how I do what I do and know what I know all comes down to making an energetic connection. Understand that you came into this world as a bundle of powerful energy, and you will exit the same way. In this respect, the living and the dead are essentially the same—both energetic bodies, packaged differently, yet made of the same stuff. A medium can communicate with the spirit world and "talk" to higher energetic beings of light by tuning in to their energy. In other words, I gotta get on *their level,* and I do this by getting into a heightened energetic state.

Understand that all energy vibrates and spins at varying speeds. The energy inside of you and me spins at a fairly slow speed because our physical bodies are heavy and dense. By their very nature, our bodies emit low energy. Spiritual energy, on the other hand, is free of physical constraints. It's easy-breezy, light, and lightning-fast. So for me to communicate with the unseen world, I must raise my energy up and access my "higher self," or pure spirit, and Spirit must slow its energy down. Once we meet somewhere in the middle, we can strike up a conversation.

Our higher self serves as a doorway to Spirit and God, and I use a variety of intuitive tools and techniques, like meditation and visualization, to heighten my energy. One of my favorite visualization practices is to close my eyes and imagine my energetic body going up, as if on an elevator. I go up and up and up, until my energy rises to a higher level. While I can get pretty high, I can never quite reach the penthouse level; Spirit has to come down a floor or two to meet me. Spirit does this by lowering and slowing down its vibration, focusing and "stepping in" to the denser energies of the physical world. This isn't easy to do, and Spirit can only sustain this lower frequency for a short amount of time. It's like pushing a helium balloon to the bottom of a swimming pool. The instant you release your grip, the balloon pops back up to the top of the surface. The more evolved the spirit, the longer it can remain at the bottom of the pool, yet it's just a matter of time before—*pop*—it's gone.

It's in between the lower and higher floors of the physical and nonphysical worlds where spirit communication takes place. I call this the "spirit level," and what I clairvoyantly see when I step off the elevator is a blinding warm white light, where brilliant bubbles float through the air. I'm usually greeted by one or more of my spirit guides and then taken to the appropriate room to meet and discuss whatever I need to know in that moment.

Maybe you're thinking, *This chick is nuts!* Believe me, when I first started this crazy work, I wrestled with a lot of self-doubt. I wondered, *How do I know that I'm not making it all up and I'm not really just a head case with an overactive imagination?* It really took years of putting my gift to the test and getting 100 percent confirmation from thousands of clients that I was indeed communicating very specific and personal messages to them from loved ones who had passed on. These days my trust, faith, and belief in the unseen world outweigh any skepticism I once had. The truth is—my human mind is just not that clever. The world that's been shown to me is beyond my limited imagination.

Exhaustion can cause us to spiritually do what we do when we're physically tired—zone out, forget what's important, and eventually nod off. This is the moment our pesky mind waits for. As soon as our spirit falls asleep, the mind seizes control. It takes the wheel and hands us a bag of chips. And because we're groggy and hungry for clarity, we gobble down every last bite of junk.

The top three lies your mind feeds you are:

> Lie #1: You are your outsides.
>
> Lie #2: You are what you do.
>
> Lie #3: You are alone and ultimately separate from the people and the world around you.

LIE NUMBER ONE

You are your outsides. Not true. In my line of work—where I can get away with speaking about things that are a little offbeat—I tell people all the time: You are more than your body. What Spirit impresses upon me time and time again is that when we die, the only thing we take with us "back home" is our spiritual energy in the form of pure unconditional love and light. Meaning, you cannot slip your impressive stock report or the deed to your house in your back pocket; our spiritual bodies don't have pockets (or fanny packs, thank you, God). The only thing you carry with you on the journey back home is the eternal light within you that *is* you.

Most people have this backward. They spend their lifetimes working hard to attain things—be it material wealth, the perfect body, status and success—when in actuality, the only thing worth anything is the wealth you cannot count or see. Instead of measuring success by how much power, popularity, achievement, and control you have, consider that success doesn't come from what you have, but rather from who and what you truly are.

LIGHTEN UP

In readings, Spirit has described to me drifting up and away from the physical body after death and going straight into a loving light. Yes, it turns out that Hollywood's version of death and the afterlife is somewhat realistic. Not only do spirits describe a Pearly Gates kind of scenario, but also many of my living clients who've had near-death experiences have also confirmed a vision of blinding white light beckoning them forth.

A client named Lindsay who suffered a heart attack and flatlined described her brief departure from her physical body as being pulled by a magnetic force toward an intensely brilliant rose garden. The garden resembled one Lindsay visited regularly in her waking life, except in this rose garden, she was greeted by her deceased mother.

Lindsay's mom had also loved roses in life, so it made sense that they'd reunite there. Mom reassured Lindsay that it was not her time to go, that her family still needed her physical presence on Earth, and she was strongly encouraged to return to her body. After flatlining for nearly five minutes, Lindsay made a miraculous comeback.

Another client who was in a severe car accident and spent three days in a coma described her near-death experience as floating freely in a warm swimming pool of white light. She remembers feeling an overwhelming sense of peacefulness, but she was nudged by "beings of radiant white light" to wake up. She described reentering her physical body like plunging into a cold swimming pool.

Spirits often tell me that regardless of how a person dies, death is a gentle, peaceful process that actually feels freeing and wonderful. Our bodies are heavy and dense, and our true state is light, unbounded, and limitless. One spirit clairvoyantly impressed upon me that death was like unzipping and pulling off a tight pair of jeans and slipping into comfy sweats. I don't know about you, but that sounds pretty good to me!

LIE NUMBER TWO

You are what you do. Also, not true. The mind loves to confuse purpose with talent. It's easy to do because they're related, but they're actually two very different things. Our purpose is to express and extend our divinity. Our special gifts and natural talent are simply the avenues through which we're able to do that. Take legendary singer and songwriter Bono of the band U2, for example. His unique voice and natural musical talent not only touch and move people, but also they enable him on a financial level to give back to those in need in third world countries. So whether he's entertaining or being philanthropic, he's using his special talent to extend God's love and light. In this way, he's living his life *on purpose.*

Likewise, you may be someone who's great at math and became a successful architect. Being naturally good with numbers doesn't mean, however, that designing homes is your purpose in life. Your purpose is to be an energetic extension of God's light and love. However you accomplish this task (and this looks different for everyone) is how you fulfill your purpose. Over and over again, Spirit assures me that in the grand scheme of things, title, position, professional ranking, and power mean nothing. In meditations and readings, spirits have clairvoyantly shown me a ladder, which is my sign for ambition and a drive for success. They've impressed upon me that the "rung" of the ladder you're on is not important. While status and success can be great confidence boosters, at the end of your life, they're irrelevant. What I've come to understand is that our true job in life is to know what we are—extensions and expressions of God—and then act accordingly. This is how we find true fulfillment. Eleanor Powell, the 1930s Hollywood starlet known for her spirited tap dancing, once said, "What we are is God's gift to us. What we become is our gift to God."

What I love most about debunking the lie that *you are what you do* is the truth that emerges from it. In group

REAL TIME, REAL WORLD: SLEEPWALKING

Sometimes we become so exhausted spiritually that we can't get out of bed, and when we finally do, we stumble around, just going through the motions, sleepwalking our way through life. I know this routine well. Fifteen years ago, my sleepwalking became a metaphor for how I was living my life.

I was a freshman in college battling a dark depression. I was unhappy with the direction of my life, feeling lost and alone. I can clearly see now that my life was off track because I felt disconnected from God; my spirit had fallen asleep. I'd forgotten who and what I truly was, and in my groggy state, I'd pursued a career path that just wasn't me. It was leading me farther and farther away from my intended purpose.

Subsisting in a prolonged state of fear, anxiety, anger, or depression can drive the best of us to adopt any number of unhealthy habits as a means to cope. And that's exactly what I did. I stuffed my depression back down my throat with food. Every night I performed a self-medication ritual of sleepwalking—or rather, sleep*eating*. At two in the morning, I'd stumble into the kitchen and carb load in my jammies.

Thirty pounds and several months later, I finally "woke up" and put a stop to my destructive behavior (for all the nitty-gritty details, read *Spirited*). Long story short, once I had my personal wake-up call, I began the spiritual mediumship work that got me back on track to fulfilling my life's divine and intended purpose—to express and extend God's unconditional love and light within me the best way I know how.

seminars, I often hear a collective "Ahhhh" from the audience when I explain that because we all possess God's love and light within us, I'm no more special, blessed, or talented than anyone else. It's just that I've identified the best way *for me* to express and extend God's love and light based on my natural gifts and abilities.

We all have the same potential to express and extend God's powerfully loving energy and light, and it starts by believing in your divine potential. It starts by believing in you. Really, being *you* is all that is expected of you. I love the classic story about the great Hasidic rabbi Zusha, who was agitated and upset as he lay on his deathbed. His students asked, "Rabbi Zusha, why are you so sad? After all the great things you have accomplished, your place in heaven is assured!"

"I'm afraid!" Zusha replied. "Because when I get to heaven, God won't ask me, 'Why weren't you more like Moses?' or 'Why weren't you more like King David?' God will ask, 'Zusha, why weren't you more like Zusha?' And then what will I say!?"

LIGHT METER

Before we move on to Lie Number Three, I want to briefly return to the idea that after you die, the only thing you carry with you on the journey back home is the love and light within you. While this is true for everyone, the *amount* of love and light we each carry varies from person to person, depending on how you lived your life, how well you expressed and extended God's love and light while in a physical body on Earth. For example, on a scale of one to ten, a sociopath is packing close to zero light, while the Dalai Lama's pushing the meter toward ten. Elizabeth Clare Prophet writes in *Kabbalah: Key to Your Inner Power* that "the soul's journey beyond her earthly life is determined by the type of devekut she pursues in her life on earth. The soul chooses her own fate." Loosely translated, *devekut* refers to how one "clings," or "attaches," to God. In other words, how brightly you shine your divine light in this world affects your passage into the next.

I work in the world of the weird every day. I freely admit that because of what I do, it's very easy for me to get lost in the clouds. I've led hundreds of audience discussions where, when I explain how the spiritual world permeates the physical world and I look out into the crowd and see glazed, somewhat confused looks, I take that as my cue to bring the discussion back down to the ground. Similarly, I realize that a lot of what I'm telling you now may sound esoteric, not tangible or relatable enough. You may be asking yourself, how does expressing and extending my "God-spark" apply to the real world? What do I *do* with this information? How do I apply it to my everyday life? How's it going to affect my upcoming lunch hour?

These are fair questions, so let me bring it back down to Earth and make it real for you. Ready?

Your true purpose in life is to become a lighter, brighter, more kind and loving spirit. That's it. It's the only reason you're here. This is what spiritual expansion and evolution is all about, and your happiness and fulfillment today, tomorrow, and in the many days ahead of you will be defined by how well you understand this truth, how well you feel it deep down, and how well you apply it to the daily grind of your life—the everyday normal and sometimes boring and ordinary circumstances. Not only that, but how you live your life today, tomorrow, and in the many days ahead will also absolutely have consequences that exceed far beyond this lifetime.

Get it?

Okay, let's pause for a seç. Take a deep breath. If you're not sure how to *be* Godly, not to worry. The simple fact that you now hold this book in your hands means you've already taken the first actionable step. You've begun the process of waking up.

LIE NUMBER THREE

You are alone and ultimately separate from the people and the world around you. If you ask me, this lie is the biggest offender. The mind easily buys into the illusion that we are separate and alone in this world, and this belief supports so many of our insecurities, defense mechanisms, and fears. The irony is that our fear is what fuels a sense of separation. But this fear is not real. What Spirit tells me over and over and *over* again is that we are all one. We are all energetically connected to one another and to God, the source of all energy, love, and light. As such, we can never be separated from one another or from God; we only *think* we can be. That's the great *maya,* or illusion, and the illusions we live through can create a great deal of pain and confusion in our lives. This is not to say that your sense of disconnection may not feel very real at times, but that doesn't mean it is. The downside to living in fear, besides how awful and vulnerable it feels, is that it hinders our spiritual growth. And when our spirits get stuck like this, our lives get stuck. Fear drives us straight into roadblocks. It escalates conflict, pain, and sadness, and it manifests scarcity. In other words, fear creates a living hell on Earth.

Over the years, Spirit has repeatedly given me from the other side validation that we do indeed live in a world of illusions. I've communicated with hundreds of spirits who express regret, frustration, and sadness over how much of their lives they spent "in hell." They wish they had understood, or at least had some sense of, their connection to God when they were still in a physical body, and yet it wasn't until they physically died and their spirits began the journey back home that it became immediately clear to them that there is no other, there is no separation. They plead with their living loved ones to wake up to this truth *now*.

Helping you to wake up to this truth is the reason I wrote this book; it's also the reason for its title. You see, deep down and *within*, you already know everything I'm telling you. I'm simply here to help you remember, to bring the behind-the-scenes knowing that resides within you—the memory of who and what you are—to the forefront of your mind.

Vernon Howard, spiritual teacher and philosopher, tells a great story about a baby lion who somehow ends up living with a flock of lambs. The lion grows up and acts like a lamb, thinks like a lamb, behaves like a lamb, until another powerful lion attacks him. Fearing for his life, he says, "Please leave me alone. I'm just a lamb," to which the other lion says, "Come here!" and drags him off to a lake and holds his face over the water so he can see his reflection. "You are *not* a lamb. You are a lion."

Huh?

The lion who thought he was a lamb stares at his refection in confused bewilderment, until finally he looks at the lion next to him and, drawing the deepest breath he's ever drawn, lets out a loud roar that terrifies the whole land. Until that moment, he never really knew who or what he was.

Much like the lion that mistakenly thought he was a lamb, most of us have forgotten our true nature, our divinity. We've strayed away from the reflective pool. Now it's time to come back and look into it anew and begin to see, and know again, who and what you truly are—a walking, talking, breathing manifestation of God.

Seductive stuff, yes? That's exactly what Narcissus thought when he came upon a pool of water and fell in love with his own image reflected there, and we all know what happened to him—he stayed mesmerized and, more or less, paralyzed by his own beauty until he finally died an unhappy, unsatisfied, and unfulfilled man. A tragedy, for sure, but the fate of Narcissus is not what I have in store for you. Rather, as you take each of the ten steps of awakening, looking further and deeper into the reflective pool until you recognize and remember who and what you truly are, you'll also discover the potential for wonderful growth and a fulfilling and meaningful existence that will ignite and light up every day of your waking life.

PART TWO

—◆◇◆—

AWAKEN

THE SIGNIFICANCE
OF THE LETTER
R

Each step of your awakening begins with the letter R. In Hebrew, this letter is pronounced "resh" and it begins the Hebrew word *Ruach ha-kadosh,* which roughly translated means "Holy Spirit." According to early mystical Judaic literature, when the letter R, or "resh," is chanted or meditated on, it's believed to awaken our spiritual senses and open us up to spiritual insights, guidance, truth, and transcendence.

REFLECT

The first step of your awakening begins with sparking your divine knowing. To do this, you will focus on the act of reflection. In other words—you'll focus on getting out of your head. Remember, the mind is a master at tricking us into believing we're alone, separate, and disconnected, from one another and from something *more*. Not true. When we turn inward and go beyond our thoughts, we become superconscious, aware of our divine essence, of who and what we really are—an energetic extension of God's powerful love and beautiful light. Through reflection, we begin to know ourselves.

Creating God awareness might seem like a rather ambitious place to start, but let me assure you there's really no other way to begin. You might be thinking, *Not so fast. Can't we solve my real, down-to-Earth problems first, like how do I find happiness and "fulfill my purpose" when I'm stuck in an unsatisfying dead-end job?* A legitimate question, and trust me—we'll get there, but before you can solve any ground-level problem, you must first tackle the Big Kahuna.

If you're familiar with traditional therapy, you know that personal issues are often approached from the outside in. You name the problem—unhappy in your dead-end job—and then you peel back the layers to reveal the deeper truth. I work in reverse. I start with naming the deeper truth and then peel back the layers, from the inside out.

This is not my particular method per se; it's just what Spirit has urged and inspired me to do. Over the years, what Spirit has communicated to me time and time again is that without first understanding, and knowing, that you're an extension of God's love and light, you'll never really resolve anything in your life, be it an unsatisfying job or an unhealthy relationship. It's only once you're empowered with this knowing, with God awareness, that you'll be able to solve your earthly problems.

So the first step of your awakening is about reflection, finding time every day to be still, so that you can not only quiet your mind, but also go beyond it. Many spiritual teachers speak about the importance of the present moment and "dwelling in the now," because it's only there that you'll find God. They're absolutely right. And the question is: How do you get there?

Becoming present starts by turning your mind chatter down. I know from years of practice that quiet, present reflection sparks divine insight. It awakens your knowing that you're a walking, talking, breathing manifestation of the most powerful energy in the universe. Reflection brings the formless into form. The infinite becomes finite.

HOW I USE THIS IN MY LIFE: BEYOND THE MIND

Quieting my mind is absolutely essential to my spiritual mediumship work. Before any private or group reading I do, I must empty my mind, like a bathtub draining water, in order to raise my energy and reach that spirit level that enables me to receive higher truths and insights. For example, this past year, I was gearing up for a major audience reading in Omaha, Nebraska. More than a thousand tickets had been sold, and I knew from past experience that for events as big as this, which are demanding just based on sheer size, it's absolutely imperative that I show up clear, calm, and totally present—meaning, my own mind chatter must be turned all the way down. If I'm at all tired, scattered, distracted, or caught up in my own drama (yes, I'm human just like you), there's no way I'll make spiritual connections. Forget about it!

Getting out of my head so that I can be a clear channel for Spirit takes work. It requires quiet reflection, and this often involves setting boundaries because we all know this: Tuning down the chatter in our own heads most often hinges on tuning out the noise around us. So to prepare for Omaha, I limited my interactions with and commitments to other people for a full twenty-four hours before the event. An hour before I was scheduled to be on stage, I kicked it up a notch and secluded myself in my hotel room; I put the DO NOT DISTURB sign on the door. I passed the next sixty minutes in silent reflection, until I was in a calm, clear, and *mind-less* state. When it was show time, I was fired up and ready to go.

And yet Omaha was a challenge. That night, the energy tugging on me from the spirit world was intense! Thousands of spirits with important messages for their loved ones were jumping up and down, wanting to be heard. People often ask me, "What do you experience and 'see' at an event like this?" What I see is a single-file line of people waiting behind a closed door. The door is my mind, and the people waiting to get through are spirits who have passed on. As soon as I remove the DO NOT DISTURB sign on that door, in effect allowing myself to be used as a clear channel between this world and the next, spirits make a mad rush to get through, sometimes fighting one another to get to the front of the line so they can be heard. If this sounds overwhelming, it absolutely can be.

Spirits don't mean to be pushy or rude. It's just that they've each been waiting a long time to talk to their living loved ones. They're eager and excited. Imagine a roomful (in this case, a stadiumful) of three-year-olds jumping up and down, all wanting your attention at the same time. They pull and tug on my energy, impressing me with thoughts, feelings, images, and sounds, and it's up to me to line them up like a preschool teacher, starting with those spirits who have the most pressing and urgent information and strongest emotional need to communicate. Once I discern which spirit needs to be heard first, second, third, and so on, I tune in to the spirits' energy and ask the rest of them to quiet down and wait their turn.

For the most part, the spirit world is pretty well versed in the basic rules of staying in line, getting along, sharing, and helping one another out. And yet, just as it is in real life, some spirits are more cooperative than others. Our personalities don't change much after we die. Our level of enlightenment reaches greater heights (more on that to come), but our essence stays the same. Meaning, if someone was pushy in life, odds are that person will be just as pushy in the afterlife. To this point, the night of the Omaha event I couldn't shake off an especially assertive spirit that kept nipping at my heels. Finally, I'd had enough! I stopped mid-sentence and said to the audience, "Time-out. Who here recently lost a golden retriever? He's barked his way to the front of the line, and until I find his owner, he's not going to quiet down."

BEYOND THE MIND

This first step of your awakening starts with ignoring all that you hear around you. That's right. To set the tone for your awakening, give yourself a little breathing room in the form of silence.

Once you're quiet, close your eyes and say the following simple affirmation:

I AM THAT I AM

That's it. *I Am That I Am.*

Your homework assignment is to recite this affirmation, or mantra, here and there and throughout your day either mentally or out loud. Say it in the shower, in the car, at the gym, walking down the street. Write it down on a

Post-it and stick it to your computer screen, or stuff it into your back pocket or purse. Whenever you think about it, pull it out and repeat it a few times.

When said out loud or inwardly, inspiring and affirming words work to lighten and brighten your energy. When you say, "I Am That I Am," you are affirming that God is where you are, that God is within; and according to many mystics, when repeated, chanted, or reflected on, this prayer releases, or *awakens,* divine knowing within you. Big promises for such a simple phrase, but believe me, I've put it to the test many, many times and I'm telling you— something powerful really does shift inside. If I'm feeling drained, distracted, overwhelmed, caught up in my own stuff, or just generally off, I'll take a moment and meditate on I AM THAT I AM to reactivate my knowing that I'm an extension of God's energy. And, really, in no time at all, I can feel a lightening and, with it, renewed clarity and purpose.

◄O►

Most recently, I put the I AM THAT I AM mantra to the test in Las Vegas, of all places. I thought, *If I can connect with God in one of the most material places on the planet, I've truly hit the jackpot.*

It was a whirlwind thirty-six-hour trip to Vegas for my cousin Lanie's wedding. She loves Vegas, refers to it as the ultimate playground, and goes so far as to call it "heaven." I, on the other hand, consider it to be hell on Earth. I don't mean to sound like a snob, but the noise level, the pollution, the intense gambling and party atmosphere, the overt materialism, and the generally toxic energy really put a sensitive girl like me in a big, bad mood. And just my luck, the weekend we traveled to Vegas was Cinco de Mayo, the popular drinking holiday most often celebrated with tequila shots. Plus, add to that, there was a heavyweight fight drawing a rowdy crowd. To say the town was nuts is putting it mildly.

The test: How do I stay centered, grounded, and connected to God and my own divinity amid the chaos?

I started by mentally repeating I AM THAT I AM in a variety of circumstances—in the hotel lobby, waiting in line for a taxi, seated among a ballroom full of wedding guests. I wasn't too weird or compulsive about it, just every so often, I'd pause and repeat the words a few times in my head.

But Vegas gave me and my simple I AM THAT I AM mantra a run for our money. Eventually the pervasive toxic energy took its toll on me. I was about to give up, or rather give in, and order a stiff one from the nearest cocktail waitress when—*poof*—my mood shifted. I felt a noticeable lightening of my energy. Throughout the remainder of the wedding reception, I felt peaceful and relaxed. Not only that, but I also had meaningful, uplifting, and even spiritual conversations with family and friends. This shift and lift in my energy put me in a position of strength and power, which enabled me to ignore all the negative mojo that is Vegas and focus in on what felt good and true.

Since making the I AM THAT I AM mantra a regular habit in my life, I've noticed that in addition to shifting and lifting my energy, it also serves to balance out the energy around me. Meaning, my divine knowing shifts the mood of the people around me. This is part of what it means to express and extend God's light and love. When you do, everyone brightens.

Pretty cool, right?

Or are you not sure you buy it?

If you're having a hard time grasping the idea that God is accessible to you, as *you*, then act as if. When you act like something already is, even if it's not yet a reality, you create a positive energetic force that draws and brings it to you. This is the basis of the Universal Law of Attraction. So if you're having a hard time believing you're energetically connected to God, try acting like you and God are old pals. Talk or pray to God like you would your bestie and see what happens. Chances are good that sooner rather than later, you'll start to sense a connection that feels solid and real.

ENLIGHTEN UP

While saying a simple mantra can have surprisingly big-time results, you'll be able to "reflect" more deeply when you throw meditation into your day-to-day routine. I like to say that meditation is just a nice way of asking your mind to shut up. Micheal A. Singer, the author of *The Untethered Soul*, describes meditation as a "return to the root of your being, the simple awareness of being aware." Edgar Cayce, the American psychic who influenced the New Age movement, likens meditation to "listening to God." Either way, meditation is simple; it doesn't require sacred space, incense, or yoga pants. The only requirement is that you set aside a few quiet minutes and then—just do it.

Most of us are busy people who resist slowing down (who has time?), so I've created a series of five-minute EnLighten Up meditations, for each step of your awakening, that you can easily integrate into your on-the-go lifestyle. As you work through the next ten steps, I encourage you to set aside just five minutes a day to dedicate to quieting your mind and awakening to your divine, radiant self, and as you do, understand that the presence of God is soft and simple. It doesn't make a grand entrance. It shows up quietly and sweetly, as subtle feelings that ripple up from deep within you.

Each of the EnLighten Up meditations is designed to unblock your spiritual and energetic body so that God's energy can flow freely through you. Remember, in our simplest form, we're just energetic extensions of God—a chip off the old block. We're free-flowing love and light packaged in a body suit. Except—when our flow of energy gets jammed, God's love and light can't move through us so well. This is what it means to feel off, blocked, shut down, distracted, drained, or depressed. Ariel, my energy healer (hey, some people have personal trainers; others see a chiropractor to get back into alignment; I have a weekly appointment with a light worker), says it perfectly: "The frequency of your energy is supposed to be a high vibration, but the Earth plain is a challenging place to be, and, as you know from experience, life can beat you up. Every time we are hit with something that we perceive as painful or difficult, [our] energy can be damaged."

For each step of your awakening, you will meditate on unblocking any damaged or stuck energy within your body, from your head down to your toes and back up again, so that God's powerful and magnificent light can circulate and flow freely through you. Again, Ariel says it best: "When this circulation of energy happens, people describe it as a feeling of floating, tingling, or expansion. They feel held in the frequency of love. This state of wholeness is what we are all trying to remember."

Make sense? Or have I gone too far out there again?

My advice: Give it a try. See what happens. You have nothing to lose, but potentially so much to gain, plus aren't you just a little bit curious?

As crazy as this may sound, each step of your awakening corresponds to a very specific pool, or center, of energy in your body. When the energy in your crown is unblocked, for example, God awareness—your knowing that God is within you, as you—is *awakened* and allowed to flow freely. In the Kabbalah tradition, crown energy is referred to as *keter,* where our divine self's knowing resides. In Sanskrit, the crown center is called the *sahasrara,* meaning "thousandfold" or "infinite." Yogis call it the "seat of enlightenment." Throughout history, saints, yogis, clairvoyants, and people who have had near-death experiences are said to radiate this crown light from their head.

I see my own crown energy when I meditate before a reading. In fact, when I clairvoyantly see and clairsentiently feel this light around my head, it means the doorway to the spirit world is open. If I have difficulty visualizing my crown energy, it means I'm stuck in my head and stuck on the ground floor with no chance of rising to the spirit level. When my crown is lit up with violet-white light, not only do I feel confident and full of grace and wisdom, but also I feel connected to higher spiritual energy—to God. This allows me to witness and observe life from a higher perspective rather than react to life with fear and confusion, which is so easy to do when our mind takes control of the wheel.

If I get pulled into personal or professional drama, I know it's better to wait until after I've meditated on the situation before I say or do anything. When my crown energy is unblocked and flowing freely, not only is my assessment of life situations more accurate, but also I'm more calm and loving.

The best way to awaken the crown is through meditation. Awakening the crown this way also *balances* your crown energy. This is important. When your crown energy is out of balance, you're off balance. You may feel fearful, separate, alone—stuck in your head, thinking too much, and as a result, alienated and disconnected from God and your higher purpose. On a physical level, you may suffer from headaches. You may feel foggy, dizzy, disorientated, and unfocused. Furthermore, when one energy center is off balance in your body, it can slow down and clog the energy pools in other parts of your body as well.

Throughout all ten steps of your awakening, your meditative work will be to unblock, awaken, and balance your entire spiritual and energetic body so that God's powerful love and light can freely flow through you.

ENLIGHTEN UP:

The Crown Is the Starting Point

Before you begin any meditation, it's important you center and ground yourself. One of my favorite techniques for accomplishing this is to focus on my breath and visualize myself as a magnificent tree, the Tree of Life, with roots extending far out from the bottoms of my feet, anchoring me in the cool, dark earth as my head reaches and lifts high, branches extending outward and upward, touching the clouds above as they pass gently by.

Close your eyes and take several deep abdominal breaths in through your nose and out through your mouth. With each breath, focus on relaxing your entire body, from the top of your head down through your toes. Imagine yourself in your favorite natural setting as a magnificent tree. Take several more deep, relaxing breaths in through your nose and out through your mouth to firmly center and ground you in this natural space.

As you continue to breathe, imagine your head reaching high into the sky and visualize a spark of violet-white light flickering just above your head, in what's called your "crown." In fact, you might imagine an actual crown sitting on top of your head, hovering just above the tip-top branches of the mystical Tree of Life and glowing with violet-white light.

Continue to breathe.

With each breath, allow this violet light to grow more and more radiant. As you continue to breathe deeply and easily, and as this violet light continues to grow brighter and stronger, expanding until it becomes a brilliant fire, set the intention to open yourself up to God's love and light. Make a promise to carry this light within you throughout the rest of your day, and let your breath serve as a reminder that you are a divine being. When you forget, repeat mentally or out loud: "I Am That I Am."

MAKE A HABIT OF PLUGGING IN

Meditation works to wake you up, kind of like your morning coffee. As it is with every sip, each meditative breath also helps you to feel more and more awake, until you're buzzing and fired up for the day. I encourage my clients, as I'm encouraging you now, to make meditation part of their day-to-day routine. The amount of time you spend in meditation is really up to you. I encourage you to set aside five minutes a day, but my personal philosophy is: Do what feels right. Some days I have the time and the luxury to stay in meditation for an hour. Other days, I wake up especially refreshed, focused, and clear, and determine that I only need a few minutes of meditation before starting my day. Either way, I leave judgment out of it. I just do what feels right for me. My only hard rule is that I carve out some amount of time every day to go inward and be still, and that's what I encourage you to do, too. Meditation is a learned practice that gets easier and better with time, so start with five minutes a day and see where it takes you. I think you'll discover that in the still, quiet, and reflective moments, your spirit rolls over, stretches, and begins to wake up.

Just as it is with my morning coffee habit, if I skip my morning meditation, I feel it. Headaches, irritability, fatigue—it's not pretty. On the other hand, when I take the time to reflect and connect with God's energy, I'm tireless. I feel light, free, and energized, like I can pretty much accomplish everything I set my mind to. Six hours of back-to-back client readings—no problem! It's kind of like how your favorite kitchen appliance works. If I want to whip up a batch of cookies for my two sons, Sam and Jakob, and I don't plug the KitchenAid into the wall, my domestic efforts are futile at best. But if I plug it in, this fabulous machine will churn out enough cookie dough to make me Mother of the Year. Likewise, when you "plug in" and allow God's energy to power you, life suddenly becomes much easier. It flows, and this is because you're energized by the most powerful source of energy that exists.

Not the domestic type? Try thinking of it this way—so long as your iPod is sitting in its dock, it'll never run out of juice, because it's constantly being charged by an uninterrupted energy source. But when you remove it from the docking station to work out to your favorite tracks at the gym, you know it's just a matter of time before the battery will slip back into the red. As it is with your iPod, you, too, have a limited supply of energy. And when you rely solely on your own energy reserve to get you through the day, the nine-to-five grind takes a lot out of you, if not everything! Over the course of the day, you wear down your battery, and by the time you get home, you're likely to feel exhausted and drained. You may feel empty, like you have nothing left to give.

The best way to avoid a red-zone moment where you

inevitably wear down and shut off is to stay connected to the source of your energy throughout the day. By closing your eyes and mentally reciting "I Am That I Am" for thirty seconds or taking a bigger than bite-sized chunk of time to meditate on your crown center, where the energy of divine knowing resides, you in effect remain "plugged in" to God, an endless supply of powerful energy that will keep you fully charged.

REAL LIFE, REAL WORLD:

Five Minutes at a Time

If spending five minutes in focused breathing and mindless thinking feels hard, that's because it is. Don't give up—keep at it. Start by setting aside five minutes a day to be still, quiet your mind, reflect, and awaken your spirit within. Once you get five minutes down, try ten, and then fifteen. Eventually, the awakened state you achieve in meditation will remain with you throughout the day.

Picking up where I left off in Vegas . . . let me share further with you how calling in God's powerful energy through affirmation and meditation shifted my energy and made what could have been a draining thirty-six hours an ultimately uplifting and validating experience.

The morning after the wedding, my husband, Brian, and I packed up to head for the airport. Downstairs in the hotel lobby the general consensus was that securing a taxi to the airport would be a nightmare. Instead of jumping into panic mode, I took a moment, turned inward, and focused on aligning myself with God's energy. I mentally asked, "God—please help me feel the connection to my own divinity and to the source of my divinity." And then I added, "Also, please make today go easily and smoothly."

Just then, right on cue, my uncle Den and aunt Ruth strolled over to us and asked if we wanted a ride. They were heading that way and could drop us off. Crisis averted! As we walked through the hotel parking lot, I noticed a license plate on a car parked right next to theirs. It read: GODISGT—God is great. I chuckled to myself. (Did I mention that I regularly receive validation, or signs, from Spirit via license plates? Kinda random, I admit, but it works. It gets my attention, and the spirits get their message across, so I've stopped questioning it.)

Thanks to the lift, we arrived at the airport with time to spare. And then, instead of being forced into a long line at security, we were waved down the first class line. Sweet! Every step of the way—through security, on the tram to our gate, and while boarding the plane, we fell in line behind a woman toting a bag with huge angel wings on it. Again, another sign from Spirit that my prayers had connected and aligned me with God's energy. Like I said, when you're connected to the most powerful energy source in the universe, life flows freely and easily.

All said, once we finally touched down in Denver, I was beat. But there's a big difference between physical fatigue and feeling completely depleted and drained. Feeling tired is a physical reality, whereas exhaustion comes from mistakenly believing you're disconnected from God and then running your own reserves into the red.

CALLING FOR BACKUP

The act of awakening your divine knowing requires devotion and a willingness to work at it. It's not a onetime event, but an ongoing, day-to-day practice and commitment. As it is with hauling your butt into the gym, some days, you might not feel up to it. That's okay. We all have days when we're unmotivated, uninspired, or unclear. This is when asking for help from those who *do* have clarity will come in especially handy.

You may have noticed my mention of angel wings in the retelling of my Vegas experience. This was not some arbitrary move on my part to add spiritual whimsy to my tale. Believe it or not, angels are constantly popping up in my life. "Of course," you say while making the universal sign for crazy. If I talk to the dead for a living, why wouldn't I also keep company with angels?

I understand that many people doubt the existence of angels. While they play a popular role in many of our favorite Christmas stories, most people don't actually believe they exist. But consider this: What if it's your belief that's unbelievable? Popular angel mythology is far-fetched, even for me. Angels are neither regular Joes hanging out at your favorite bar, cherubic babies flying around in clean diapers, or white-winged Victoria's Secret models perched high up in the clouds.

Are you willing to update your current understanding of what an angel is? Great! I'm so glad you're open to new ideas.

In their purest form, angels are highly evolved spiritual beings of divine light. They're like us; they're extensions of God's energy. Except, where we contain only sparks of God's love and light, angels are burning bright with it. They're like blind-your-eyes radiant, and their spiritual energy is off the charts.

Angels are spiritually enlightened beings whose power and purpose is to oversee our earthly lives and help wherever they can to make them run without a hitch. Sometimes this is accomplished by inspiring a thought to spur us into action; other times they lend us superhuman strength when we're feeling weak. They often impress us with feelings of comfort and clarity, and sometimes they show us literal signs, confirming that we're not alone and our lives are on track.

It takes courage and a big shot of humility to yield to higher guidance—angels, no less. Yet, if you're fumbling your way through darkness, feeling lost and looking for the light at the end of the tunnel, I encourage you to open yourself up to the idea that unseen forces are working on your behalf. It's this angelic guidance that I've come to rely on when doing readings for clients, especially in big group settings like the one in Omaha I described earlier. Remember how I equated the spiritual energy in the room that evening to a stadium of three-year-olds all jumping up and down wanting my attention? You may have read that and thought, *Ick, that sounds horrible, and why would I want advice from a three-year-old having a tantrum, anyway?* Like I said before, spirits don't mean to be pushy, demanding, or obnoxious; they're just excited to communicate with their living loved ones and want badly to be heard.

Thankfully, accompanying these spirits are higher

enlightened beings of light. They clairvoyantly appear in my mind's eye as balls, spheres, and orbs of light, and these angels and guides are the ones who help me filter through all the information coming at me. Basically, they help me cut through all the chitchat so that I can hone in on what's most important. They help me interpret and deliver what I call "higher truths," from the spirit world to the living.

Angelic guidance is available to all of us at any time—not just woo-woos like me. Spirit has assured me that whatever the issue, whatever the problem—really, there's nothing too big or too small—an A-list team of angels is waiting in eager anticipation to work with each and every one of us. Over the years, angelic beings of light have shown up countless times in my dreams, meditations, and readings offering help and support. Consistently, I clairvoyantly see angelic beings in my mind's eye, reaching out their arms with their palms open. I've clairaudiently heard them say, "Call on us; ask us for help. Remember to shout aloud when you feel alone. We will help and work with you as we may." I've clairsentiently felt their light and loving presence when reading clients, as if they're standing just off stage, waiting for their cue to enter. From my experience, what I believe and know to be true is that angels are ready and willing to jump into our lives and lend support as soon as we say, *Help!*

In addition to relying on mantras and meditation to get God's powerful energy moving through you, feel free to call on different angelic guidance to walk beside you each step of the way. For each step of your awakening, I provide you with a specific archangel to call on to help unblock

CAN I EARN MY WINGS?

Some of my more spiritually ambitious clients want to know: "Can I earn my wings?" The answer is *not necessarily,* and anyway that's not what this book is meant to teach you to do. The ten steps of awakening are meant to encourage you to, and show you how to, become the highest expression of God's love and light in this lifetime, and while this is a noble goal (in fact, it is *the* goal), it won't necessarily qualify you for angel status.

You see, angelic beings are super-evolved. Think of them this way—they're the left and right hands of God. And because their energy is so light and bright, and spinning and vibrating off the charts, they cannot physically be contained in a fleshy human body. It's impossible. So in terms of earning your wings, I suggest leaving angelic aspirations to the angels. Your work today, tomorrow, and the day after that is simply to move forward, learn, grow, and be the best human you can be.

your spiritual and energetic body, so that God's powerful and magnificent energy and light can flow freely through you. These specific assignments are not arbitrary; they're based on Kabbalistic tradition, and my Kabbalah teacher in Denver, Dr. David Sanders, was a big help in this. As angelic guidance relates to the first step of your awakening, there's one angel in particular who's associated with great inner change, who specializes in waking us up to our divine knowing. Does that seem odd—that within the spiritual realm there are specialists? Well, if you have a plumbing issue, you call the plumber, not the doctor, right? Just as people have different areas of expertise to help you in different situations, angels do, too.

As a conduit of crown energy, Archangel Akatriel is the guy to call to awaken your divine knowing that God is within you, as you. Akatriel is best for this job because— hands down—he's considered to be the most powerful of all the archangels. His name means the "crown of the source of the whole of existence." He's sometimes also called the "great crown judgment prince placed over all the other angels" and the "Angel of the Lord." He's kind of a big deal. He's referred to as the link between God and humanity. In other words: He's the closest thing to God's powerful energy, so he's really the best angel to call on to help you awaken your connection to the Divine. Archangel Akatriel gives us the gift of clear thought, which helps open our minds to seeing beyond who and what we think we are.

In meditation, Archangel Akatriel appears to me as a larger-than-life character, an angel with a crown on his head, radiating white and gold light. His powerful energy not only leaves my head tingling, but also takes my breath away. I feel almost starstruck by his presence, like you would be if you ran into God on the street. Really, it's *that* profound. I never take his presence lightly, because his energy tends to correspond with spiritual transformation— big-time inner stuff.

TEAM SPIRIT

Throughout the ten steps of your awakening, you'll be introduced to many high and mighty angels to call on for guidance, but you should know that your support system doesn't stop there. Just as you probably have many friends and family members you can turn to in times of need, you also have a team of enlightened spiritual beings that have your back. It took me several years to get familiar with all the angelic and spiritual guidance available to me and to understand their special purpose in our lives. The biggest challenge for me, as it no doubt will be for you, was to trust and believe.

In meditation with Spirit, I've been clairvoyantly (with clear seeing) and claircognizantly (with clear knowing) provided with the following understanding of spiritual rank and order:

Archangels

These angels are God's MVPs. They hold the highest rank in the angelic realm. As you can imagine, they're busy, but you can call on them at any time and they'll drop what they're doing and lend you a hand. Seriously, they're *that* powerful. They can assist millions of us at the same time.

Guardian Angels

We each have one or two dedicated guardian angels that are with us from birth until death. Their job is to oversee our lives, to keep us on track and out of harm's way. They're pretty much at our beck and call; so don't be afraid to call.

Angels

In addition to our guardian angels who watch over us and keep us safe, we each may have a scattering of other angels assisting us from time to time. Within your lifetime, you may have sensed this warm and loving angelic energy around you, felt it guide you or help you heal during troubling times. Angels are very inventive. They send us signs and arrange coincidences, or "synchronicities," as a way of letting us know that we're on the right path. Angelic guidance is free and available to you 24/7, so I encourage you to take advantage of it.

Ascended Masters

Ascended Masters, also called the "Masters," are powerful healers, teachers, or prophets who previously walked upon the Earth and know well the hurdles and setbacks that life often presents to us. I'm talking about guys and gals like Jesus, Mother Mary, Rachel, Quan Yin, Buddha, Sathya Sai Baba, and Ganesh. In the spiritual realm, the Masters are the overachievers. They lived and loved hard, and now they've graduated to a much higher level of being, while the rest of us humans are still back in the fifth grade.

These loving and calming energies represent many different creeds, castes, and colors, and yet anyone can call on them. Yes, anyone. The Masters are simply not interested in conversion; it makes no difference to them what your religion is. Collectively, they lovingly work together from the spiritual realm to open our hearts, bring healing, wisdom, and guidance to those who sincerely call upon them, and assist humanity and the planet in loving service.

Spirit Guides

Spirit guides are enlightened spirits who have *been there, done that*—meaning they were once human.and now they're between lifetimes, taking a break from physical life and working from the other side to guide the living. They're like trusted best friends, teachers, and mentors, and they come and go throughout our lifetimes depending on our level of need and what particular period of adjustment they've been trained to guide us through. At any given point, we may have several "visiting" and "permanent" spirit guides working on assignment to help us meet particular challenges. Notice I said help, not solve. They can't take away our challenges, but they can offer us thoughts and feelings of comfort and clarity to help us work our way through them. Once their work is complete, they kiss us good-bye and move on to help someone else.

Deceased Loved Ones

These are the spirits of our loved ones who have left the physical world and now inhabit the spiritual world. They're still present in our lives, acting as cheerleaders to inspire us. At some point, our deceased loved ones may take on a guardianship role, but not before going through extensive training on the other side.

Incarnated Beings of Light

These are living, breathing people who seem wise and enlightened beyond their years. They are commonly referred to as "old souls," and most of us know people like this, whose energy tends to both calm and uplift us and whose actions inspire us to *be more*. These are children and adults who have been here before. They've returned once again, leaving the spirit world for the physical world, with the gift of clear insight and higher knowledge to help and heal the planet.

In extreme cases these highly evolved incarnated beings of light feel different, like they don't fit in. They may even feel that they don't really want to be here on Earth and would rather go "home"—a phenomenon known as divine homesickness.

PLACING THE CALL

If after trying the I AM THAT I AM mantra and crown energy meditation, you're still feeling stuck in your head, disconnected, and doubtful that you're anything more than a bag of flesh and bones, call on Archangel Akatriel. Say aloud or just think: *Akatriel, please be with me. Please help me to remember my divine radiance and help me to feel connected to God, the source of my divinity.*

Again, understand that archangels are busy. They will not interfere in your business unless you ask them to, so you have to ask. The Universal Law of Free Will requires us to initiate and invite in outside help. That said, no need to make it complicated or formal. Place the call anytime, anywhere. In the shower, in the elevator, as you're making dinner—as long as your request is heartfelt, Akatriel will answer your call. Also know this: When it comes to angelic presence and assurance, it's generally not an in-your-face experience. It's something you *feel*.

REAL LIFE, REAL WORLD:

Suspend Disbelief and See What Happens

My friend Aliza, who's totally open to what I do but not necessarily into practicing it herself, texted me one afternoon about how stressed she was at work. She wanted to know: "Rebecca, do you have any advice?" I thought, *You asked for it,* so I texted back, "Would you consider asking Spirit for help?"

I held my breath waiting for a reply. I imagined her rolling her eyes at my response, but again—she was well aware whom she was asking for advice. A few minutes later, and to my pleasant surprise, she texted right back, "How?"

I responded, "Just ask your angels and guides, either mentally or out loud as if you were talking to me or another good girlfriend. Tell them what you need help around and thank them for anything they can do to lighten your workload and stress."

She then asked, "How do I know I'm talking to my angels and not inviting in dark and spooky spirits?"

I replied, "So long as your intention is pure, you have nothing to worry about. You're always in control of what you let in, based on your own energy. Be the light you want to attract, and darkness will have no spell over you. Darkness is *dispelled* by light." Later that day she texted back: "You win. I asked my Team Spirit for help and—no joke— two things were resolved today! Work issues that have been so stressful and unresolved forever were cleared up. I'm amazed! Literally, I asked for help this morning and then help came my way WITHIN HOURS!"

I smiled when I read her text. Funny how when you reach out and ask for what you need, you almost always receive a helpful hand.

reflect: A RECAP

- Through reflection, by turning inward and going beyond our thoughts, we become super-conscious, aware of our divinity, of who and what we really are—an energetic extension of God's powerful love and beautiful light.

- When you say, "I Am That I Am," you are affirming that God is where you are, that God is within.

- In addition to repeating the I AM THAT I AM mantra, reflect more deeply by meditating on unblocking the energy in your crown, so that God awareness can flow freely.

- In the ancient Kabbalah tradition, the expression of our divine self's knowing is referred to as *keter,* as its energy resides in our "crown." When crown energy is unblocked and awakened, expect to feel a new level of awareness of who and what you truly are.

- Angelic guidance is available to all of us at any time. For a conduit of crown energy, call on Archangel Akatriel to help awaken divine knowing.

STEP 2

RESET

Once you've begun the practice of quiet reflection, ask yourself, *Is my life on track? Am I living my life on purpose?* If you're not quite sure, then it's time to reset the connection to your divine navigation system—that is, your intuitive wisdom. Since you are an energetic extension of God, it stands to reason that within you is a powerful supply of God-like wisdom. Not only is this a reasonable assumption, it's actually true, and when you "reset" and tap into this wisdom, suddenly the direction you need to take next to fulfill your life purpose becomes a lot clearer.

What you might not know is that in addition to your five physical senses—hearing, sight, touch, smell, and taste—you also have a sixth sense: innate wisdom, also called intuition. We each come into this world armed with a strong sixth sense, but then, almost as soon we're born, we start to ignore, mistrust, and second-guess it. Most of us have second-guessed our intuitive wisdom for so long, we've forgotten it even exists, and then we wonder why we feel so disconnected from ourselves, lost, confused, uncertain about what our life's purpose is. Well, the good news is that you can change all that by simply *resetting* your intuition. And once you do, you can expect a familiar sense of clarity, like an old childhood friend, to return to your life. As you begin to spend time with your old pal, trust and rely on her or him, you may be tickled to discover that the world is much easier to navigate. With your intuition reset, the road ahead begins to snap into focus, and with this clarity comes the confidence to redirect your life.

So the question is: How do you reset it?

It's simple, really. Listen to your feelings.

I like talking about feelings, because everyone has experience with them. You're likely to have always had some sense of what you feel about someone, something, or someplace. *I feel threatened. I feel cold. I feel comfortable.* Sometimes you might just feel "off." When you can name your feelings—that is, be really honest with yourself about what does or doesn't feel good—you identify what's true to you, you at your very core, and this is what tapping into your intuition is all about. In other words, you listen to yourself in the most basic way.

When you listen, and I mean *really listen* to your feelings, it's like dropping a pin on the map of your life. Your feelings will tell you exactly where you are. They'll also tell you how best to get from point A to point B.

REAL LIFE, REAL WORLD:

Inside Out, Not Outside In

For many of us, the religious and cultural beliefs we grew up with were so strong and persuasive that we stopped looking *inside* ourselves for wisdom and guidance. In other cases, the opinions and voices of our parents were so overpowering we stopped listening to, and trusting, our own. In my childhood home growing up, my intuition was far from nurtured. In fact, it was criticized. As a kid, I had an active mind, conversed daily with imaginary friends (what I later understood were spirits), and I was supersensitive to the energy of the people around me. My dad, whom I adored and looked up to, teased me for being "too sensitive," so in an effort to please him and win him over, I did everything I could to silence my intuitive voice. Little good it did me. It was too loud to be shushed. Eventually, after many years of stuffing my voice down, it finally screamed—*Listen to me!* As I write about in detail in *Spirited*, resetting and starting to trust my intuition constituted the beginning of my awakening.

When you stop looking for direction outside yourself and instead reset and tap into your intuitive wisdom to make the best day-to-day choices, from what to order for lunch to bigger and more important life decisions—like *Should I stay in this relationship or my current professional field?*—the answers will become clear. Personally, before I make any decision—and yes, this often includes what I put on my lunch plate—I always check in with my intuition first.

OH, WHAT A FEELING

Set the intention now to go within and quiet your mind. With a quiet, reflective mind, ask yourself, *How do I feel? Do I feel good? Do I feel uplifted? Does my life feel on track, or is something off with me or a situation I'm in?* Your feelings and emotions are your strongest indicator if your life is moving in a purposeful direction or not, so listen closely to how you feel and pay attention to whatever comes up. If you're a particularly visual person, you might try imagining a white chalkboard or a blank movie screen and after asking the question *How do I feel?* watch what *appears.*

Usually, when we can't shake a particularly uncomfortable or foreboding feeling, when something doesn't feel right, it's our divine intuitive wisdom telling us that either a situation we're in or a person we're involved with is not in our highest or best interest. Meaning, we've strayed off course. We've taken the wrong exit, and the more we fail to listen to and honor our feelings, the longer we'll continue down the wrong road.

My son Jakob will often ask me, "Mommy, what should I do?" I tell him, "Ask your feelings. How is the situation making you *feel*?" When he had a falling out with a friend at school who'd called him a hurtful name, he came to me wanting advice. Jakob explained that he thought he should probably just let it go, keep the peace, play nice. I said, "Okay, that's what you *think* you should do, but how do you feel?" He said, "I don't feel good, Mommy." I gave him a hug and said, "Honor your feelings. Maybe he's not the best friend for you."

SHAKING IT OFF MAY SHAKE YOU UP

We all know people who ignore their feelings—usually it's because they don't take them seriously, they're embarrassed by them, or they just *don't want to deal*. And yet if you ignore your feelings, they far from disappear. They manifest in often weird and unhealthy ways. Case in point: My husband, Brian, went through a particularly difficult time with his dad a few years ago. Mending their relationship would mean a lot of work, which Brian wasn't ready to do. He was in denial. Dealing with his feelings felt too hurtful, so what did he do instead? He started compulsively shopping online. Specifically, he started buying Nike shoes for our then eight-month-old like they were going out of style. More than *fifty* pairs of baby Nike Air Jordans later, I put it together: He was self-medicating with our credit card. I encouraged Brian to really listen to his feelings, as uncomfortable as they might be, and work on mending his relationship with his dad. Also, I added, "Feel free to list all fifty pair of those baby Nikes on eBay." *Really*—babies who don't walk yet can't jump!

This story is a good example of what happens when we ignore our feelings. We often self-medicate with drugs, alcohol, or other distracting behaviors, like overeating or shopping, when what we really should be doing is honoring how we feel.

REAL LIFE, REAL WORLD:

Out of Touch?

Sometimes we're not sure how we feel about a person, circumstance, or situation. My best advice in these instances is to do a gut check. Pretend you're at the doctor's office going down a medical checklist of symptoms—in this case, *feelings*—and mark the ones that apply to you and the person, circumstance, or situation in question. Ask yourself, *Do I feel sad? Angry? Anxious? Numb? Jealous? Tired? Frustrated? Afraid? Depressed? Apprehensive?* Or conversely, *Do I feel happy? Excited? Content? Calm? Uplifted?*

Before you do or do not check the box next to a particular feeling, take a deep breath and sit with it for a moment. Remember, your breath gets you out of your head, allowing you to reflect and receive intuitive guidance. As you sit with each emotion, ask yourself if it's relevant. For example, *Do I feel sad?* Is this emotion relevant to the situation? If sadness doesn't elicit a reaction within you, chances are good that you don't feel that emotion. Trust me, when you hit one that *is* relevant, you'll know it because you'll be flooded with more of that same feeling.

LISTEN AND TRUST

The key to listening to your feelings is *trusting* them. Unlike our minds, our feelings do not lie. Yet even I still struggle with this from time to time. I, too, have to be ever vigilant about quieting my mind and trusting my divine intuitive wisdom. For example, my husband and I recently decided to take our son Jakob out of private school and enroll him in a nearby public school. As soon as the decision was made, we started hearing from friends and neighbors about how difficult it was to get into this particular school. Most often, you cannot be rejected by a public school, but we'd heard that because it was at capacity the school was turning away students trying to "choice in." I arrived home from work one afternoon and Brian was all worked up. He'd talked to another neighbor and was totally convinced we'd prematurely pulled Jakob out of his current school without knowing "for sure" that he'd get into the neighborhood public school. I said to him, "He's in. I'm not worried about it." But Brian thought otherwise, so he pressed me: "Ask your guidance, what does it say?" I closed my eyes and asked for an answer: *Will Jakob be accepted?* While your intuition most often speaks directly to you through your feelings, it also delivers information through insights, revelations, and urges. In this case, my intuition definitively said, *YES!* This made Brian feel better and we dropped the subject.

Until.

Later that evening, I was out to dinner with a girlfriend and we started talking about the school issue, and all of a sudden, doubt flooded *my* mind. I started to think, *Maybe he won't get in.* Worry, fear, and stress crept in where knowing had been before. Over the course of our dinner, I could feel my energy weaken (fear will do that), and by the time I got home, I couldn't wait to join Brian in his doubt, "What if you were right? Now I'm beginning to think that

Jakob won't get in." I spent the next couple of hours before bedtime questioning my own divine guidance. The next day, I frantically e-mailed the principal for an answer, and when I received a reply it simply said: "Jakob has been accepted."

So what's the moral of the story here? When divine intuitive wisdom—that is, strong *feelings*—whisper in your ear, listen up! I would have saved myself a lot of needless panicking if I'd only done what I'm telling you to do now: trust and stay solid in what you know.

HOW WILL YOU KNOW?

I say that, and yet maybe you're wondering—*How will I know that I know?* Good question. Allow me to make the distinction between a mind thought and intuitive wisdom. Mind thoughts tend to piggyback on top of one another, where you think of one thing, which leads to another thought, and another and another. You may think you've been hit with divine intuitive wisdom, but when you trace your thoughts back, you discover that they were manufactured by your mind. For example, you drive to work, you spot a dog that looks just like your brother's dog, you think to call your brother. This is a trailed mind thought.

Meanwhile, an intuitive thought really does come out of nowhere, with nothing attached to it. Also—and this is key—intuitive thoughts tend to repeat as strong feelings and urges *until acted upon*. For example, Sandy, a girlfriend of mine who'd spent the majority of her young adult life working as a nanny, started to wonder if she might be able to take her skills to another level. *But how?* she wondered. *What would I do instead?*

A week or so later, while she was making dinner, a thought struck her—*What if I become a maternity concierge* (an advocate and consultant for expectant parents) *like Rosie Pope on the Bravo show* Pregnant in Heels? But prone to self-doubt as so many of us are, Sandy dismissed the idea as too far-fetched. She put it out of her mind. Except the next morning, there it was again. She couldn't shake the feeling that she was on to something. For days, this potential new career path continued to creep into her consciousness, and then, when a friend of hers who knew nothing of her recent call to pursue something more, sent her a link to a class that would certify her to become a maternity concierge, she thought, *Okay, this is getting weird!* Still, she laughed it off and tried to dismiss the "coincidence." But by the very next morning, she was all but obsessed. She couldn't get the class off her mind. "Fine," she conceded out loud and called the online registration number. The woman who answered was happy she'd called—there was just one more space available and the class was starting that day! Did she want to sign up? This was the final validation, or sign, that Sandy needed. She resolved that pursuing a career as a maternity concierge was the direction she was meant to go.

What many of us don't realize is that *the signs are always there.* Meaning, intuitive wisdom—that which gives us clear answers and direction—is always available to us, within us. As you become familiar with how your intuition works, you'll begin to recognize divine intuitive guidance directing you forward in your day-to-day life. It's almost

REAL LIFE, REAL WORLD:

The Difference Between a Mind Thought and Intuitive Wisdom

- A mind thought is trailed, where one thought leads to another, then another, and on and on and on. Intuitive wisdom crashes in from out of the blue.
- A mind thought can sound whiny and child-like. Intuitive wisdom often sounds more wise and grown-up.
- A mind thought feels foreign and out of character. Intuitive wisdom feels familiar and right.
- A mind thought speaks to you in the first person— I. Intuitive wisdom speaks in the second person— you.
- A mind thought is often fleeting. Intuitive wisdom is repetitive and consistent.
- A mind thought can feel cold, critical, fearful, and competitive. Intuitive wisdom feels warm, empowering, purposeful, and loving.
- A mind thought is often focused on the past or the future. Intuitive wisdom is felt in the present moment.
- A mind thought procrastinates. Intuitive wisdom takes action.
- A mind thought is short-lived information. Intuitive wisdom is supported by a series of synchronistic events.

as if as soon as you suspend doubt and disbelief and open yourself up long enough to the possibility that signs will guide you along, they'll appear just when you need them.

In my day-to-day life, I know it's my mind making noise if I'm rehashing a situation or a conversation fifty times in my head, using critical, defensive language like a child trying to get her way. The cool thing about learning how to differentiate between intuitive wisdom and mind thoughts and then choosing to *trust and act on* your intuition over the often unreliable mind is that the more you do it, the more validation you'll get that your intuition is your best guidance forward.

ENLIGHTEN UP

For this second step of your awakening, you'll again meditate on releasing any clogged or stuck energy within your energetic body that may be inhibiting you from accessing your divine intuitive wisdom. In case you've forgotten, meditation is just the act of quiet and reflective deep breathing. You can do the following meditation anytime, anywhere so long as you're in an environment where you can quietly inhale and exhale undisturbed for a five-minute chunk of time.

When the pool of energy located within your inner eye is opened and unblocked, your intuition is similarly awakened. In the Kabbalah tradition, divine wisdom, or *chokmah,* resides in the inner eye. Referred to as the "third eye" in dharmic spiritual traditions, particularly Hinduism, it's thought to be a gate that leads to inner

ENLIGHTEN UP:

Open Your Eyes

Close your eyes and take several deep abdominal breaths in through your nose and out through your mouth. With each breath, focus on relaxing your entire body, from the top of your head down through your feet. Imagine yourself in your favorite natural setting as a magnificent tree, roots grounded firmly in the earth, branches reaching high up to the sky. Take several more deep, relaxing breaths to firmly center and ground you in this natural space.

Once you feel centered and grounded, focus on your "inner eye," the space just above your eyebrows, in the center of your forehead. Imagine your inner eye nestled high within the uppermost branches of the Tree of Life. Imagine opening this eye. Visualize it staring back at you. Now imagine a spark of indigo blue within your inner eye. With each breath, allow this intense indigo light to grow more and more radiant, until it becomes a brilliant flame.

Continue to breathe.

Set the intention now to reset your innate wisdom, your divine intuitive guidance. Make a promise to keep your eyes open throughout the rest of your day, and let your breath serve as a reminder that divine wisdom resides within you. If you forget or doubt this, repeat mentally or out loud: *It is safe for me to rely on my intuitive wisdom, to see what I need to see in this moment in order to move forward.*

realms and spaces of higher consciousness. In New Age spirituality, an open third eye often symbolizes a higher state of enlightenment.

If you're someone who easily and regularly remembers your dreams, it's likely the energy centered at your inner eye is already open and unblocked. My son Jakob's inner eye is wide open, and he expects everyone else's to be, too. He's developed a pretty adorable habit of saying to me, "Mommy, look at what happened today at school," and he'll close his eyes, scrunch up his forehead, and touch it to mine. He'll say, "Do you see?" He's convinced that if we touch foreheads he can shoot me a vision and telepathically show me what's in his head. You and I know it doesn't really work that way, but the truth is—it *does* work that way in the spirit world (minus the forehead touching). Spirits communicate by swapping mental impressions, thoughts, and feelings back and forth, and this is what Jakob's trying to do. When he touches his forehead to mine, he's actually trying to communicate with me just as he would have in the spirit world, before he was born into his little boy body on Earth.

Since everything starts energetically and over time manifests emotionally and physically, if your inner eye energy is blocked or out of balance, not only will you find it difficult to clearly assess your life, but also you may feel creatively blocked. Inner eye energy is linked to the creative right brain. On a physical level, if your inner eye energy is out of whack, you may suffer from sinus and vision problems.

REAL LIFE, REAL WORLD:

Be More Childlike

Most children are naturally led by their intuition because it feels natural. And it is! It's how we each communicated before we were born into a human body, and since children haven't been here for all that long, following their intuition is automatic behavior for them.

Your intuitive sense is like a muscle. The more you work it, the stronger it becomes. For as long as a child's intuition is nurtured, it will continue to stay strong. I once read a woman named Carrie, whose mother came through in spirit. Mom, who'd died several years earlier, communicated that she often visited Carrie's three-year-old daughter (her granddaughter), who could clairvoyantly see and clairsentiently understand her. I explained to Carrie that if she nurtured and encouraged her daughter's divine intuitive sense, she and Carrie's mother could maintain a meaningful connection long beyond the grave.

CALLING FOR BACKUP

As you continue to strengthen your divine intuitive wisdom, don't be afraid to ask for help. Remember, you have a team of spirits at your beck and call who are more than happy to help guide you forward. Even I need the occasional reminder that my team spirit is out there, watching, listening to, guiding, and supporting me. On days when you're similarly feeling lost, directionless, or even just the slightest bit foggy, ask for guidance. Specifically, call on your guardian angels to help you see your life more clearly and find the answers you've been searching for. Ask them to show you signs of their presence and then be open to receive what messages they have for you.

GUARDIAN ANGELS

We each have at least one dedicated "guardian" who's been with us since birth and who will stand at our side until our physical death (that's a commitment, and more than most of us can say for many of the people in our lives!). Our guardian's job is to oversee our lives, help us stay out of harm's way, and guide us toward fulfilling our life purpose. It's a big job, and our powerful guardians are more than equipped to handle the task.

PLACING THE CALL

In addition to asking your guardians for clarity, you may also call on Archangel Peliel to give you guidance. According to Kabbalistic tradition, Archangel Peliel mentored Jacob, the Old Testament patriarch who's considered the father of the people of Israel. His name means the "wonderment of God." In my meditations, Archangel Peliel appears to me as a very serious professor with strong masculine energy. He's like the college prof whose lectures were so commanding and magnetic he was able to silence a room simply by clearing his throat.

Now, understand that I've been calling on the higher spiritual realms for a long time, so don't expect Archangel Peliel to strut right into your consciousness and give you a lecture as soon as you place the call. Nor should you expect your experience to look and feel quite like mine. Enlightened spiritual beings communicate with most people through inspired thoughts and subtle feelings. With practice, time, and trust, though, as you awaken and develop your intuitive wisdom, don't be surprised if you're better able to receive and interpret more specific spiritual guidance. For now, just think or say aloud: *Guardian angels and Archangel Peliel, please be with me. Please help me to see clearly. I'm calling on you now to help me reset my intuitive wisdom, my divine inner guidance. Help me to trust and follow my intuition to guide me forward in big and small ways.*

REAL LIFE, REAL WORLD:

Intuitive Guidance Put to the Test

During my morning meditation, I was clairvoyantly shown a bookstore at the same time I felt a strong urging to go there. I wasn't sure why I was being given this guidance, but I filed it away with the intention to remain open to it. Later that morning, on my drive to the gym, I remembered there was a Borders bookstore directly across the street. I really didn't want to cut into my workout time, but the same strong urging I'd experienced during my morning meditation was back. I made a promise to myself that if the same urging were still with me at the end of my workout, I'd head over to the bookstore. And what do you know? An hour later, the urging had transformed into a full-on mental assault—*get over there now!*

As soon as I entered Borders, I was overcome with the presence of a male spirit who directed me toward a man in the Mind, Body, Spirit section (go figure). The man looked up at me as I approached, and I made some idle small talk. I pointed to a book by James Van Praagh and said, "I really like that author." The man responded that his mother had two of the author's books. And then it was time to cut to the chase. I said, "I know this might seem weird, but I communicate with the spirits of deceased loved ones. I just left the gym across the street and something told me I needed to come in here. This is weird for me, too. I don't usually approach perfect strangers, and I don't mean to freak you out, but did your dad just pass recently?" He told me that his stepdad had just died, and I said, "I think I'm supposed to talk to you."

After a series of clear validations, I was able to prove to this man that his deceased stepfather was present with him. I clairaudiently heard his name, Al, and clairvoyantly saw him shaking his head, which is my sign for regret or disappointment. I felt the sense of clear knowing that his regret was tied to how he'd treated his family. I told the man in the bookstore, "He wants you to know that he is sorry, that he didn't do right by you when he was here, he did not treat you right." I added, "He also knows about George. Does this mean anything to you?"

At this point, tears started to flow out of this man's eyes. He confirmed that Al had been an alcoholic, verbally and emotionally abusive to the entire family. And, in fact, he and his mother had argued over Al's leftover "bad energy" the night before. He also confirmed that his mother had a new boyfriend whose nickname was George.

I said, "Al is showing me that you and your brother shouldn't worry about your mother. George will protect your mom." I then felt Al's energy pulling back and fading away. The intensity of his spirit lightened, and the information coming through from the other side started to fade until there was nothing. Suddenly, I was back in my own head, feeling quite clear and calm. Before I turned to leave, I left the man with one final message, "When you go out to your car, sit quietly and focus. If you have more questions for Al, he will try to help guide you as best he can." And with that, I left Borders, hopped into my car, and thanked Spirit for giving me such awesome opportunities to put my intuitive wisdom to the test.

reset: A RECAP

· When you stop looking for direction outside yourself and instead rest and tap into your intuitive wisdom, the answers will become clear.

· Usually, when we can't shake a particularly uncomfortable or foreboding feeling, it's our divine wisdom telling us that either a situation we're in or a person we're involved with is not in our highest and best interest. Meaning we've strayed off course.

· Intuitive wisdom—that which gives us clear answers and direction—is always available to us, within us. The more you trust and act on your intuition, the more validation you'll get that it's your best guidance forward.

· In the ancient Kabbalah tradition, the expression of divine wisdom is referred to as *chokmah,* and its energy resides in the inner eye. When *chokmah* energy is opened and allowed to flow freely, expect to feel an awakening of intuitive guidance.

· As you continue to strengthen your intuition, don't be afraid to ask for help in seeing your life more clearly. For a conduit of *chokmah* energy, call on Archangel Peliel to give you guidance and help awaken your divine wisdom.

RECOGNIZE YOUR ROLE

As you become more intuitively aware of where you are on the road of life, it might help to know how you got here. Understand that where you've been, where you are now, and where you're headed are a result of either your steady, exceptional, or reckless driving. Meaning, if you're not happy with where life has taken you so far or if you're feeling frustrated and stuck in the intersection you sit in now, you have no one to blame but yourself. While this might sound a bit harsh, when you realize that you're the driver behind every event and circumstance in your life, you also come to understand that you have absolute power to change the direction of your life at any time.

This next step of awakening is about recognizing the role you've played, and are currently playing, in creating the life you have now. Set the intention to spark further insight into your life by developing and fine-tuning your inner vision. And when you do, you'll come to understand that the people, events, and situations that have shown up yesterday and today are not mere happenstance. Rather, you requested their presence.

The question is: How?

BY INVITATION ONLY

You've already begun the work of resetting your intuitive wisdom, and the most compelling reason for doing so is that the decisions and choices you make on a day-to-day basis will become less and less influenced by your fearful mind. You see, the thoughts and visions you repeat in your mind every day work like an invitation, where what you think about most will eventually become your waking reality. This doesn't necessarily have to be a bad thing, except for the inconvenient truth that most of us approach life from the dark corners of our mind, where envy, anxiety, self-doubt, and fear like to hang out. I call this "our icky place," and what you should know is that this place is not real; it's a creation of your mind, and yet over time, the longer we spend time there, the more real it actually becomes.

Financial struggles, relationship strains, and health issues are most often the eventual manifestation of negative thoughts. Understand that when you approach life from a limited perspective—*I'm not good enough, smart enough, pretty enough; I'll never fit in; I'll always be overweight, broke, alone, unhappy*—not only will your life feel incomplete, deprived, and unsatisfying, but eventually it will look that way, too.

A client named Jason is a perfect example of how limited thinking can *become* reality. When Jason was a young boy, his father tragically hung himself. He was raised solely by his mother, who was emotionally absent, always struggling financially, and resentful of her parental obligation to her son. As you might imagine, Jason grew up a pretty sad, lonely, and fearful kid. By adulthood, he'd adopted a "poor me" attitude toward life. He believed he would always struggle financially, that people could not be trusted, and that the world was generally unkind.

But then he met a kind woman who cared deeply for him, loved him unconditionally, and also had a boatload of money. Triple score! From the outside, it appeared that Jason's luck had finally turned around. Except Jason didn't see it that way. He continued to think and act like a wounded victim. His attitude evolved from "poor me" to truly entitled. Surely, he thought, the world owed him for all that he'd suffered as a child. Instead of appreciating his good fortune, he abused it. He quit his job, sat around the house, spent his wife's money, and self-medicated with drugs. For years this went on, until finally, his wife had had enough. She cut him off financially, separated their bank accounts, and eventually filed for divorce. As far as Jason was concerned, this turn of events was just further proof that he'd always be poor, that people could not be trusted, and that the world was unkind. Yet, in truth, Jason really had no one to blame but himself. It was his thoughts, attitude, and actions that determined how his life story had played out. This is exactly how the Universal Law of Cause and Effect works—every cause has an effect, and every effect has a cause.

OWN IT

When you step back and look at your life, understand that much of what you see—the people, circumstances, experiences, and situations—has shown up in response to your mental invitation. Good or bad, I encourage you to be accountable for what you've invited into your life. Own it. And if you don't like what you see, determine to change it. You have the power to create a different reality for yourself by continuing the practice of reflection, quieting your mind on a day-to-day basis and allowing your intuitive wisdom, rather than a limited mind perspective, to guide you forward. While taking your intuition's lead requires faith and trust, I hope you can recognize that you have a choice in how you experience your life. Abundance or deprivation—you decide. Sarah Ban Breathnach, author of *Simple Abundance,* says it well: "Both abundance and lack exist simultaneously in our lives, as parallel realities. It is always our conscious choice which secret garden we will tend."

Eva had lost her sister to cancer, and she came to me hoping I'd help relieve her grief. When I opened myself up to be a channel for Spirit, Eva's deceased mother came through right away, and not to console her, but to dish up a plate of tough love. By clairsentiently impressing me with feelings of criticism and harsh judgment where I actually felt beaten down, Spirit helped me understand that Eva had never felt good enough, that she believed her parents had always favored her sister. I was also shown that Eva overate as a way of punishing herself for being inadequate. When I asked Eva about the validity of these impressions, she admitted that she'd always struggled with her weight and was currently self-medicating with food to assuage her grief over her sister's death. At five-foot-three, she weighed over 250 pounds, so her mother was rightly concerned and her message to Eva was simple and direct: Pray for a change in perception. I explained to Eva that her limited, self-sabotaging thoughts were throwing her off track from fulfilling her life's purpose—to express and extend the divine and radiant love, light, and beauty within her. I suggested hypnotherapy and daily affirmations to help her reprogram her thoughts. I told her, "If you could see yourself through God's eyes rather than your limited mind's eye, you'd be more compassionate and empathetic toward yourself, and less judgmental and punishing." Eva's mother in spirit urged her daughter to take responsibility for her "fat," "ugly," and "unlovable" thoughts and recognize that they were creating her unhappy reality. As incentive, Mom clairvoyantly showed me two people coming together and holding hands—my symbol for soul mate—and promised Eva that a man was waiting for her, but that Eva had to turn her thinking around before she'd attract him to her. This excited Eva and gave her motivation to change course.

To help you remember that how you think determines much of your waking reality, I suggest a simple and symbolic practice I created years ago. Take a book out of your personal library and cover it with a brown paper bag, as you may have done in high school to protect your textbooks. On the cover write your name in big block letters as the author of your story. This practice is to symbolically remind you that you are the author of your life. Set this book out in plain sight for you to regularly see and acknowledge that you alone write your past, present, and future.

IT'S IN *YOUR* CONTRACT

While much of your present day reality is a reflection of what you think most about, there *is* another force at work determining how your life story unfolds. Over the years, Spirit has communicated to me the same message countless times: Before being born into a physical body, we each scripted, or contracted, certain life lessons, challenges, and events to show up along the road to serve as opportunities for us to learn, grow, and spiritually evolve. Remember, spiritual evolution *is* your life's purpose, and each of us is born with a unique plan for fulfilling it.

Get this—over the years, I've communicated with thousands of spirits who confirm the same thing: We each come into this life with unique abilities and natural talents for expressing our divinity and extending it to those around us, and we're also each born with a contract, a list of predetermined challenges to *test* our divinity. In this respect, each of our lives is designed to be challenging.

That you don't remember drafting this contract for your life is no accident. There's such a thing as "TMI" when it comes to remembering our past lives, life between lives, and knowing what we contracted for this lifetime. Think about it—can you imagine as a baby being burdened with all this information? No doubt, that would give you something to cry about! If we each came into our physical bodies with full remembrance of the other side and what we're meant to tackle on Earth, we'd just want to go back "home," where our challenges and work aren't so arduous and where it's round-the-clock, feel-good love and light. To avoid this inevitable homesickness, we each go through a spiritual detox of sorts before being born, in which our memories of the past and the upcoming events of our lives are purged from our system. In this way, we can start over. We can begin again.

You see, we can learn and grow exponentially faster on the Earth plane; there's no better classroom to learn in, and this is why we choose to come here. While we can choose to continue our growth in the spirit world, it tends to inch along at a much slower pace. We're simply not presented with the same transformative experiences and opportunities that we have on Earth, to accelerate our spiritual growth in a relatively short amount of time. Also, in a physical body we have access to our six senses, which allow us to experience life with greater intensity. Consider this analogy: You can talk and daydream all day long about traveling to Europe. You can research Paris museums, read novels set in Italian villages, watch documentaries, and study German history, but none of that compares to the actual experience of getting on a plane and *going there*.

Knowing it's just a temporary ride, our spirit courageously chooses to leave the comfort of the spirit world and jump back into the often harsh, heartbreaking, and draining physical world. Only in this way can we have the full experience of living, learning, and spiritually evolving. Note: It's always a choice, and one where we choose the body, economic and societal situation, and family dynamic that will best support the lessons we need to learn to spiritually grow and fulfill our purpose. So if you catch yourself feeling like a victim or taking on a "poor me" role, drop it; your life is by design.

Your contract is largely based on lessons you failed to learn in the past and new challenges you decided to take on this go-round. I've worked with many clients who are experiencing a particularly rough ride—chronic illness, the tragic death of a loved one, significant financial loss, painful relationships, addiction—and when I deliver the news that they likely contracted these events to show up in their lives, they think I'm cracking some kind of cosmic joke. When I assure them it's not part of my stand-up act, I've had clients say to me, "Well if that's the case, what the *hell* was I thinking? I must have had some sick sense of humor when I dreamed up my life!" If you feel similarly, what Spirit assures me is that we only sign up for what we can handle. And the truth is: Some of us can handle a lot more than others. Everyone's path is different. Regardless, take comfort in knowing that as difficult or impossible as your life may seem to be, you set yourself up to succeed, not fail. Elisabeth Kübler-Ross, the Swiss-American psychiatrist and author of *On Death and Dying*, in which she first discussed her theory of the five stages of grief, said, "The most beautiful people we have known are those who have known defeat, known suffering, known struggle, known loss, and have found their way out of the depths. These persons have an appreciation, a sensitivity, and an understanding of life that fills them with compassion, gentleness, and a deep loving concern."

WHAT'S YOUR RETURN POLICY?

A colleague of mine once joked about my understanding of reincarnation. He said, "If I'm spiritually enlightened enough to know that I need to go back to Earth to do the right thing, then I've already reached a certain level of enlightenment, right? So why do I need to go back?" My answer is: greater challenges, more growth and enlightenment. Despite what you may have been led to believe, reincarnation is a great opportunity, not a punishment. It provides us with an awesome and unparalleled occasion to do better and *be* better, and because most of us are overachievers (you know who you are), the reality is that one lifetime on Earth often isn't enough to get us where we want to be. Most of us must live through a number of physical lifetimes before we're light, bright, and enlightened enough that we can opt out of a return to Earth. And then some of us return anyway, to serve as guides and teachers, an example of what it looks like to be energetic extensions of God. These spirits return to Earth and take one for the team, so to speak (more on these guys and gals later).

That said, not every spirit chooses to reincarnate. If they all did, who would I talk to? Joking aside, there are an infinite number of spirits, and while many reincarnate, many do not. Reincarnation is not a spiritual requirement. We have free will in the spirit world, too, and we decide how we want to further our spiritual growth. Some of the more advanced and enlightened spirits make the choice to stay on the other side, acting as mentors to support and prepare younger spirits planning to take the plunge back to Earth.

Earth is a classroom where we set up situations to test ourselves. To this end, each of us is born with different struggles and strengths that both hinder and help us pass these tests. For example, you may struggle with relationships and job anxiety, while your sibling or best friend battles with addiction and health issues. You may excel at demonstrating patience and listening to others, while your coworker is naturally skilled at motivating and leading. Your stability and stumbling blocks are going to be unique to you, based on the lessons you need to learn in this lifetime to become lighter, brighter, and closer to God. Each of us learns differently, at our own pace, and yet we're all trying to achieve a similar goal, which means one should not judge and compare one's life with another.

A client named Joan had a good friend named Debbie. They lived in the same small town they'd lived in for thirty years. They'd raised their children together and had always been close family friends. Over the years, Joan's kids moved away and her marriage failed. The divorce hit her hard financially, forcing Joan to work until retirement age. Joan did not have the extra time, energy, or money to see her kids or grandkids as often as she'd have liked. This saddened her.

Debbie, on the other hand, was still married to her husband of forty years, was extremely wealthy, and all but one of her kids lived in the same town. If she wanted to, Debbie could spend every day with her children and grandchildren. She didn't have to work and often vacationed with her kids and grandkids.

As you can imagine, Joan was a little jealous of her girlfriend. Sometimes, she even felt angry with Debbie, especially during long recounts of all the "wonderful times" Debbie was having with her kids and grandkids. Yet Joan bit her tongue. Debbie was her friend, after all.

When Joan came to me for a reading, her deceased father came through immediately. He clairsentiently impressed me with feelings of resentment and clairvoyantly flashed me an image of my best girlfriend, my sign for female friendship. Not knowing about her and Debbie's relationship, I asked Joan, "Is there a friendship with another woman that's making you feel frustrated or burdened?" Joan told me everything I just told you about her and Debbie. Through a series of images, feelings, and a sense of clear knowing, Joan's deceased father communicated to me that Joan and Debbie had signed up for two different paths in life to learn very similar lessons. While Debbie seemed to have it all, she secretly struggled with chronic health issues, as did two of her daughters. Dad explained that she'd "contracted" her physical struggle to be an example of bravery for her kids and grandkids. Joan's struggles, on the other hand, were more financial, and yet her lesson to learn was the same—to be an example of courage and strength, proving to herself, her kids, and her grandkids that she could rise up after falling. Both women were meant to leave behind a similar legacy.

Joan's father wanted his daughter to see the bigger picture, as he saw it now, and to recognize that both women had contracted different ways of reaching the same goal. Dad encouraged Joan to let her resentment go and to, instead, pat herself on the back for doing such a wonderful job at achieving what her spirit had intentionally set out to do. At the end of the reading, Joan said she was grateful for finally recognizing that she and Debbie were mirror reflections of each other, both strong and capable, no better or worse.

What Spirit has shown me time and time again is that we each choose careers, experiences, and relationships based on what our spirit needs to learn to become more loving, kind, full of light, and God-like in this life. These lessons differ from person to person and we take on individual roles to learn them. To fulfill my purpose, I'm a teacher and a healer. You may be a natural caregiver or a leader. Our lessons to learn and the roles we play are what make each of our lives unique, yet at the end of the proverbial day, we share the same goal.

RISE OR FALL

On a deep level of understanding, you already know that the life you're living today is a temporary ride and that any obstacle in your path is simply an opportunity to shine. That said, many of us fail to rise to the occasion. Given the choice, which is what the Universal Law of Free Will is all about, most of us take what seems to be the easier road, not fully understanding that when we avoid the life lessons that show up as obstacles in our path, we only temporarily dodge them; it's only a matter of time before life serves them up again. Understand that the lessons you've contracted to learn will continue to resurface throughout your lifetime until you face them head-on. While the details—who, what, when, and how—are subject to change, the overarching lessons will remain the same.

For example, a girlfriend of mine has a habit of getting into one strained, painful relationship after another. Her most recent boyfriend is the victim type. He's clingy, jealous, and suspicious of everything she does. And while I wish she'd just dump him already, I understand that on a spiritual level, he's her teacher. She's not to blame him for making her unhappy, because he's shown up with a purpose—to challenge and test her divinity. Energetically, he's poking holes in her bright bubble of divine love and light, and the question is—will she stand up and rise up, or will she fall flat by continuing to allow him, and the next boyfriend after that, to deflate her? Either way, the choice is totally *on her*.

When clients come to me who are unhappy, confused, or stuck, and who say things like "I feel like I'm driving in circles," or "Every decision I make feels like a dead end," I know that on a spiritual and often unconscious level, they're avoiding or running away from an important life lesson. My work is to help them wake up and recognize what that lesson is. From there, it's 100 percent up to them to decide if they want to do the work in order to learn and grow, to spiritually evolve.

THE CHOICE IS YOURS

We each have free will, which means that just because you contracted a particular life lesson ahead of time doesn't mean you'll actually learn it. You have the freedom to do as you please. The choice is yours. Now, don't get me wrong,

I'm all for personal choice, but our free will, along with our human tendency to overthink rather than intuitively *feel* our way through life, can often drive us into brick walls.

A client named Bonnie came to me looking strung out and unsettled. To remain objective, I don't like to know anything about a person or his or her situation before I read that person, so I didn't ask Bonnie what was troubling her. I just sat down and called in her spiritual guides. Immediately, both her father and brother came through in spirit. They clairvoyantly showed me a woman in between Bonnie and her husband, combined with a clairsentient feeling of betrayal and secrets. I said, "Your guides are telling me your husband is cheating on you." Bonnie indeed had her suspicions, and this confirmed it. As anyone would be, she was devastated. Her father and brother impressed on me that she seek support, and also confront her husband.

A week later, Bonnie returned for an emergency reading. She was in a desperate place. When I called in her guides, her brother came through in spirit again with a stronger and more urgent plea: *Leave him now; he will never change his ways.* I was clairvoyantly shown an image of her husband running in place, which is my symbol for being stuck and unlikely to change. I said to her, "I know you don't want to hear this, but your brother is saying: Walk away before you completely lose yourself. There's hope if you have the courage to do your part and face this situation, learn from it, and move forward with your life." She cried for a long time and confided in me that after being married for forty years, she was afraid to leave her husband. He'd given her two healthy and happy kids and financially provided for her in a way she feared she couldn't replicate on her own. Spirit asked me to reassure her that she *was* strong, and that she should do what was best from a spiritual perspective. In other words—confront the lesson and move on. Bonnie heard all this, but when she left my office that day, I intuitively knew she wasn't going to leave her husband. She wasn't going to follow the guidance, and as a result, she'd continue to suffer from her choices.

Over the years, Spirit has communicated to me that our lives are a marriage between free will and predetermination. We're born with a script, a contract based on what our spirit needs to learn in order to grow and evolve, but what actually plays out depends on our choices, our free will. In readings, spirits regularly acknowledge that the choices they made in life threw them off course, stalling their spiritual growth. Once they died and reviewed their life, they realized they could have done better. Frustrated and regretful, they recognize that their work is not done and they'll eventually need to return to Earth's classroom and *do it all over again*. Again, this is what reincarnation is for—another chance to make better choices, grow, and evolve. Spirits plead with me to help their living loved ones wake up and remember that passing life's tests is the very reason for being here, in your body, at this time. This is what I mean when I say: Recognize your role, and realize how you're playing it. Take responsibility for the life you're living. You created it. You chose it. When you accept that events, situations, and people are not flukes, but quite intentional, and when you embrace challenges with the intent to resolve them, rather than resist them, you'll jump back on track to living your life on purpose.

Gale lost her twenty-two-year-old daughter to a car accident. She came to me for a reading hoping I would help her make sense of it all. As Gale took a seat across from me, I looked into the face of a woman whose spirit seemed already to be gone. It was like looking at a ghost—displaced energy drifting in between this world and the next. It was eerie, actually. Almost as soon as I closed my eyes and called in her guides and deceased loved ones to give me clarity and messages, Gale's daughter in spirit came through, impressing on me that her mother was contemplating suicide. Spirit used my personal frame of reference to communicate Gale's feelings and desperate intention. After the birth of my second son, Sam, I experienced postpartum depression and sunk to a place so low I came to understand what suicidal thoughts feel like. While reading Gale, I felt a wave of that same old desperation wash over me. I asked Gale, point-blank, "Are you thinking about hurting yourself?" Gale burst into tears. Just that morning she'd considered taking her own life.

Her daughter impressed on me that her mother was holding on to her grief unnecessarily, and that she wasn't seeing the bigger picture—the divine purpose of her daughter's death. Gale's daughter wanted her mother to know that she was at peace, and she impressed on me that her untimely death was actually *right on time*. On a spiritual level, it was to serve as a test for her mother to draw on her own reservoir of strength and not succumb to grief, anger, and the kind of hopelessness that can lead to suicide. Her daughter urged her mother to embrace this life lesson, to open up her heart and heal, and trust and have faith that her daughter's death was not in vain. Her daughter was rooting for her, hoping that her mother would recognize that her daughter's death provided her with an opportunity to grow, eventually reuniting the two of them in the spiritual realm. She warned that if her mother took her own life, she'd escape nothing. Her lesson to learn would follow her into the next lifetime. Gale's daughter urged her mother to connect the dots and do the necessary work to evolve through her grief.

SOME THOUGHTS ON SUICIDE

Many of my clients come to me confused about suicide. They want to know: Is suicide part of one's "contract," meaning, does one actually sign up to take one's own life prior to being born, or is the act of suicide strictly an act of free will? I've wondered about this, too. Both my grandmother and my father committed suicide. I've asked my guides this very question many times. Here's what I understand to be true: Suicide is not predestined. It's an act of free will.

Spirits who've committed suicide have expressed to me that while it wasn't their contract to die in that way, they came into life with the *potential* for suicide; they were predisposed to suicide either because of a hereditary chemical imbalance or because another family member or a peer took his or her own life, making suicide an unconscious plausibility, a path to also follow. Either way, what Spirit tells me is that committing suicide is always an act of free will, and by making this choice, these spirits inevitably find themselves on the other side facing the same difficult work they left behind on Earth. In short, they're back where they started.

Think of it this way: A person who commits suicide is not unlike a student who's struggling in school and decides that instead of pushing through, he or she would rather give up before the semester is over. And just like the dropout who cannot advance to the next grade or level without first going back and re-tackling and passing the difficult course work, someone who commits suicide—and, in effect, drops out—must also return to the classroom of life and finish his or her work before he or she can advance to the next spiritual level.

I've connected with hundreds, if not thousands, of spirits who have died by taking their own life. In fact, a large majority of my readings involve consoling people who've lost a loved one to suicide. These spirits are drawn to me because of my very personal experience with and sensitivity to suicide. They sense that I don't judge them, but rather have sincere compassion for how they struggled in life. These very spirits routinely express their regrets for not reaching out to the support available to them in both the physical and spiritual worlds. If only they'd reached out and asked for help, perhaps then they'd have resisted the temptation to drop out of school and throw it all away. Sadly, there's a stigma attached to mental illness, and most spirits admit they failed to ask for help out of the shame and guilt of possibly being associated with it.

While the loved ones of those who commit suicide can

regard the unfortunate loss as an opportunity to learn and spiritually grow in their own lives, I want to be clear—there are no winners when it comes to suicide. I know this, and have felt this on a very personal level.

My father, Shelly, killed himself when I was thirty years old, and it's been the saddest event of my life. Within the first year of his death, I really struggled with whether or not his death was part of his contract or an act of free will. At the time, I spoke with many colleagues who do the kind of work I do who suggested his death was part of his contract to help *me* develop my intuitive gift. This never rang true with me. I couldn't accept that his death was all a play to propel me forward.

Today, I can now objectively see that his death was clearly a matter of personal choice. Dad has come to me in several intense dreams, called "visitations," where he's expressed unbearable grief, regret, and heartache over the finality of his choice. While Dad's tragic death undeniably intensified and clarified my life's work and path, I believe I was destined to do what I do regardless of my father's actions in life. His life choices ultimately affected *his* spiritual evolution, not mine. Dad has also visited me countless times in meditation and shown me that to make his suicide "right" in terms of karma, he's working with the spirits of kids and young adults who have also died in a similar way, helping them connect with their living loved ones through me.

In one powerfully intense dream, I witnessed a young man lighting himself on fire. I woke up in a sweat! Two days later, at a large group reading in Denver, I was clair-voyantly shown another flash of the same horrific scene and clairaudiently heard the name "Mike." In my mind's eye, I also saw my dad standing to the side of this spirit, helping him to make a connection with me. I asked the audience, "Does anyone know a Mike that died by suicide . . . something to do with a fire?" Sure enough, Mike's mother jumped out of her seat, along with two other family members sitting to the left and right of her. We went into a very moving and profound reading where I connected Mike's mother with her son, and the whole time I could see my dad standing in the corner of my mind's eye with his arms crossed, wearing a confident and proud grin. I claircognizantly knew Dad was proud of the work we were both doing, helping the living and the dead heal, find closure, and feel at peace.

WHAT ROAD ARE YOU ON?

So, now that you realize that *you,* and not other people, circumstances, or events, are driving your life experience, how do you identify which road you're on—the one you've mentally attracted or the one you've contracted? And does differentiating between the two even matter?

The answer is, not really. But if you're curious, here's how to figure it out. Take a quiet moment now to awaken a deep understanding and realization of the role you're playing in your life. On an energetic and spiritual level, the following EnLighten Up meditation works to unblock and release any confusion you might have around a situation you may be struggling with by awakening and clearing the energy in your inner eye and throat center.

In the ancient Kabbalah tradition, the light of God's vision is referred to as *binah,* and, like *chokmah,* its energy is centered in the inner eye. How we see the world is determined by how fluid and free-flowing this energy is within our body. In Sanskrit, this energy is called *ajna,* which translates as "command." In the Hindu culture, it's believed that a healthy and open inner eye gives us command over our lives and, with it, the ability to manifest what we envision. If it's blocked, our perception will likely become distorted and negative, often resulting in an urge to control people and outcomes.

ENLIGHTEN UP:

Steady Your Eyes and Clear Your Throat

Close your eyes and take several deep abdominal breaths in through your nose and out through your mouth. With each breath, focus on relaxing your entire body, from the top of your head down through your feet. Imagine yourself again in your favorite natural setting. Do you know where this is? Imagine it now and take several more deep, relaxing breaths to firmly center and ground you in this natural space.

As you continue to breathe, imagine yourself as a magnificent tree, with your head reaching high into the sky and your feet rooted into the earth below. Again, visualize an indigo blue light flickering in your inner eye, within the uppermost branches of the Tree of Life. As this light flickers and begins to expand, recognize that you have the power to see all situations, events, and people in your life from a broader perspective; set the intention to see yourself through God's eyes. What is life trying to teach you?

Continue to breathe.

Now visualize this swirl of flickering indigo-blue light as it leaves your inner eye and travels down into your throat where it lightens into the color of a calm blue sky. Breathe in this gentle blue light. Feel it expand in your throat center. Think of a situation you may be struggling with and wish to find clarity in. Set the intention to realize what role you're playing in this situation.

Throughout the rest of your day, let your breath serve as a reminder that you're an extension of God's powerful love and light, and as such, divine vision and understanding reside within you. If you forget or doubt this, repeat mentally or out loud: *I choose to see every situation in my life through God's eyes, gaining greater perspective, clarity, and appreciation for all that is.*

The energy centered in your throat relates to personal responsibility and realization and kabbalists call this *da'at*. If energy isn't flowing so freely through your throat center, you may find it difficult to clearly articulate and express yourself. As a result, you may feel misunderstood and victimized, and you may hold grudges. A healthy and open throat, on the other hand, means you're no longer blaming others for your struggles and challenges. When your throat is open, you're much better able to take full responsibility for your life. An open throat is also related to one's ability to create and manifest abundance. Think about it—once you stop the blame game and realize *It's not about* them, *it's about* me, once you take ownership of the events, circumstances, and relationships in your life, you reclaim your power.

WHAT'S THE THEME?

After you've spent no more than five minutes meditating on awakening and releasing the energy centered at your inner eye and throat, ask yourself, *In what area of my life do I need illumination so I can see the bigger picture? In what area of my life am I failing to recognize my role?* Once you determine the area in your life that feels off, take a step back and consider whether or not your current struggle is a recurring theme in your life. While you consider this, I'll share with you one of mine.

Since as long as I can remember, I've been an emotional eater. In college, I ate as a means to numb and stuff down my feelings of depression and misdirection, and while I'm in a much happier place today, from time to time I slip back into my old unhealthy habits. I eat when I'm stressed, tired, or weighed down with other people's energy, both the living and the dead. I know better, but after a long day of work, kids, and household chores, self-medicating with sugar is a big temptation, and a great distraction! Not only have I spent a great deal of time over the years praying for freedom from my dysfunctional relationship with food, I've also asked the question: What's the lesson here? What is my issue with food trying to teach me? And the answer always comes back to this: Stop turning to an external source like homemade chocolate chip cookies for comfort, company, and soothing in challenging times, and turn inward instead, where God's healing love and light already reside—and in abundance no less.

So let me ask you—what do you think you signed up to learn? Take a look at your life. Do you notice any themes—that is, similar situations or people that continue to pop up over and over again? If so, chances are good that they've shown up to teach you something important. On the other hand, if you look at your life and the detours and the dead ends don't appear to be thematic, and meanwhile your day-to-day demeanor is most often described as sulky, surly, or sad, you've likely attracted your current life to you by thinking negatively, and you will continue to attract more and more unwanted situations, people, and events into your life until you put the brakes on and consciously turn your thinking around. All this said, whether or not your current life is the one you've contracted or attracted doesn't really matter, because either way, you can change course in an instant, so what direction do you want to go?

WHAT DIRECTION DO YOU WANT TO GO?

While it's true that roadblocks are an inevitable part of life, what Spirit confirms for me on a daily basis is that life is intended to be harmonious and synchronistic, easy even, full of magical moments and joy. So if life feels hard for you, like you're running into obstacles every-where you go, consider this a red flag signaling that you're off track and there's a better direction to go. If a current situation or relationship is not serving you—meaning you don't feel good, happy, or peaceful—then I suggest taking an "I'm over it, and I'm getting *on* with it!" attitude. The key to doing this is to turn your attention away from what is not serving you and what doesn't feel good, and focus your attention on what will serve you and what does feel right and good. What you focus on expands. So rather than complain, critique, analyze, and judge where you are on the road of life, take a minute to quietly pull over onto the shoulder and refocus your thoughts, time, and energy on the direction you'd *like* to go. And then before you get back on the road, repeat after me:

> *I accept that I'm the creator of my life, and I forgive myself for getting detoured from my intended purpose.*
>
> *Everything unfolding in my life is an opportunity for me to learn and grow. When faced with tragedy or challenging times, I surrender all resistance that stands in my way of seeing and learning a valuable life lesson.*
>
> *I take full responsibility for how my thoughts have shaped my reality. I recognize the love and light in me; it's always been there, and now I see it.*

CALLING FOR BACKUP

As you continue to strengthen your inner vision and recognize the role you're playing in your life, call on the angelic realm to walk beside you along the way. While your tendency may be to run away from dealing with the tough, rough, and challenging times in your life, this is the ultimate reason for the human experience—to face and embrace the life lessons we each signed up for, and the moment we do so, our guides and angels raise a banner of triumph for us. If you're struggling, I encourage you to ask the spirit realm for help in taking an honest inventory of your life, and for the courage to make the necessary changes to do and be better.

What many of us often forget is that when we scripted our current life, we invited our guides and angels to help us along the way. While Spirit can't remove any obstacles in your path (that would defeat the purpose of you

ANGELS

In addition to your dedicated guardian angel who specifically watches over you and keeps you on track, we each may have any number of garden-variety angels assisting us within our lifetimes. You may have sensed the presence of these angels around you, felt them guiding and healing you. As higher spiritual beings, angels have some pretty cool abilities, such as arranging coincidences or "synchronicities" to get our attention and sending us signs to help guide us forward.

contracting them in the first place), Spirit can offer you subtle thoughts and feelings of comfort and clarity to help you best work your way through them. When all is said and done, however, Spirit must honor your free will and stand back while you make your own choices and decisions.

PLACING THE CALL

In addition to calling on your angels and guardians, specifically call on Archangel Jophiel (kinda sounds like "jovial") to help you recognize the life lessons being presented to you and realize the role you're playing in your day-to-day life. Archangel Jophiel is often referred to as both the "Beauty of God" and "Divine Beauty." This angelic energy can help you recognize the lessons that have purposefully, and often quite beautifully, shown up in your life. In art, Jophiel is often depicted holding a light, representing her work illuminating and inspiring people with beautiful thoughts. In more modern times, people have often called on Archangel Jophiel to overcome the ugliness of addictions and unhealthy thinking. You'll know Jophiel is assisting you if, when searching for answers about the direction of your life, you all of a sudden experience flashes of insight in which everything becomes clear. When I'm feeling restless or anxious about how a situation is unfolding, I'll call on Jophiel, and almost immediately her soft and gentle presence calms me down. On days when you're struggling with doubt and fear about your future, or when you need a current situation resolved, call on Archangel Jophiel. Remember, your angels and guides surround you at all times. You need only acknowledge their presence and invite in their help. Say aloud, or just think: *Archangel Jophiel, please be with me. Please fill my heart with forgiveness and help me to see clearly. Please help me see through God's eyes and make choices that will positively benefit everyone involved.*

THE SIGNIFICANCE OF 11:11

Does this ever happen to you? You just so happen to glance up at the clock or look down at your watch either at work, in your car, at home, or out and about and it's precisely 11:11? This happens to me all the time, and what I've been told by Spirit is that 11:11 is a sign; it's one of the rather quirky ways in which our spirit and angelic guides wink at us, in an attempt to get our attention. When you see 11:11 (and no, waiting for it by watching the clock doesn't count!), consider it a nudge from the angelic realm to be mindful of the life you're creating moment to moment. In numerology, 11:11 is two master numbers side by side, representing illumination. When I happen across 11:11, I understand this is my guides' way of saying, *Pay attention! Recognize that life will continue to offer you opportunities to fulfill your contract and live life on purpose. Every day, it's your choice to make!*

recognize: A RECAP

· When you step back and look at your life, understand that much of what you see—the people, circumstances, experiences, and situations—has shown up in response to your mental invitation.

· While much of your present day reality is a reflection of what you think most about, there is another force at work. Before being born into a physical body, we each scripted, or "contracted," certain life lessons, challenges, and events to show up along the road to serve as opportunities for us to learn, grow, and spiritually evolve.

· These lessons will continue to resurface throughout your lifetime until you learn them. Our lives are a marriage between free will and predetermination; how our lives play out depends on our choices, our free will.

· In the ancient Kabbalah tradition, the expression of divine vision is referred to as *binah,* and its energy is centered in the inner eye. How we see the world is determined by how fluid and free-flowing this energy is within our body. Likewise, the energy centered in your throat relates to personal realization and kab-balists call this divine expression *da'at*. When your throat is open, you're able to take full responsibility for your life.

· As you continue to strengthen your inner vision and recognize the role you're playing in your life, call on the angelic realm to walk beside you along the way. For a conduit of *binah* energy, call on Archangel Jophiel to give you the courage to face and embrace the life lessons you signed up for.

RESIDE IN LOVE

Now that you recognize your role and understand that the life you're living is a creation of your thoughts and that the people, events, circumstances, and challenges that show up on your doorstep are most often disguised lessons you're meant to learn in order to grow and spiritually evolve—what now? Where do you go from here?

At the risk of sounding very cliché, your work now is to reside in love—that is, infuse loving-kindness into everything you do. Beginning today, set your intention to shine your divine light and love onto every person you meet, every situation you're a part of, and every place you go. Believe it or not, this one simple gesture will turn your life around and propel it forward in ways you cannot imagine.

When you think loving thoughts and approach people and situations with kindness and respect, you'll discover, and quite miraculously I might add, that the inevitable bumpy roads ahead will suddenly become much easier to navigate. In other words, when you *reside in love,* your life flows easily, just as it's intended.

Case in point: My car was making strange noises and running rough. In fact, it had been acting cranky for a while, but the last time I took it in to the dealership, the mechanics more or less told me I was imagining things; they didn't detect anything wrong with the car. While it is true that I hear and see things that the average person does not, I knew that I was not making these noises up. So I took the car back in to the service department, except this time, before I walked into the building, I sat in my car for a few minutes to meditate. I visualized a bubble of love and light surrounding me, my car, and the mechanics on duty. I evoked a feeling of gratitude for the issue being resolved easily and effortlessly.

I then walked in, explained my situation, and asked if I might drive around with the mechanic to point out the noise I was supposedly making up in my head. I received no push back. In fact, they agreed that this was a great idea! As soon as the mechanic got in the car with me, I made a point of asking him his name and how his day was going. This is something I've learned from my socially outgoing husband. Brian always takes the time to genuinely connect on a personal level and express appreciation and respect to anyone whose help he's asking for.

After twenty minutes of driving around, not only did Dan the mechanic hear the noise I heard, but also we'd struck up a conversation about raising kids. He opened up about his prematurely born two-pound baby who had heart issues. I took the opportunity to tap into my intuitive sense and reassure him that his son would be perfectly fine despite his rocky start in life. He seemed grateful for the reassurance and gave me his word that he'd spend as much time as needed to resolve the issue with my car. Since the fix could take more than a day, Dan offered me a loaner vehicle—one of the brand-new floor models straight out of the showroom. Sweet! Dan said loaning brand-new vehicles wasn't common practice, but for some reason, he wanted me to have something really nice to drive around in. Naturally, I was grateful for the loaner and also validated that because I had taken the time and set the intention to go into the situation with an attitude of loving-kindness, Dan mirrored it back to me by granting me his favor and respect. As an added bonus, my car was fixed and returned to me within twenty-four hours. I'm telling you—when you reside in love, the road of life is much easier to navigate.

FILL UP FIRST

Extending love, kindness, and respect outward starts with awakening it from *within*. The truth is: You simply can't give away what you don't already have. So to reside in love, you must love and respect yourself first. Remember, spiritual work happens from the inside, out.

Treating yourself with loving-kindness begins with acknowledging that your divine essence, what you're fundamentally made of, is God's unconditional love and light. What Spirit has communicated to me time and time again is that without first understanding, and knowing, that you're a unique individual expression of God, you won't be able to successfully extend God's love, which is what your life's work and purpose is all about. We must each come to the deep realization that God is love, we are God incarnate, and therefore we are love. This goes back to step one, where every time you say, "I Am That I Am," you're affirming that *God resides in me, as me.*

Several years ago I had an out-of-body experience when I was under general anesthesia. I saw a cloud of white light and felt this incredible energy pulling me toward it. When I woke up, I was sure I'd heard the Beatles song "All You Need Is Love" playing throughout my surgery. When I asked my surgeon about the background music in the operating room, he looked at me like I was nuts. That's when I realized that in my altered state, my spirit had left my physical body and traveled to the spiritual plane, where I was reminded of this simple truth: *Be kind. Be love. In the end, love is all that's real.*

If you're still struggling with actually believing that you're an energetic extension of God's powerful love, or if you're unwilling to accept it, take a deep breath, quiet your thoughts, and consider this: On a deep level, you know what you are. You know where you came from and what you're made of. It's your pesky mind that has you thinking otherwise. Again.

Need I remind you that it's your mind that tells you that you are your outsides, you are what we do, and you're alone and separate from the world around you? Take a moment right now to imagine each of these lies floating inside of a thought bubble. Now take a pin and pop each one of them. *Pop. Pop. Pop!* Doesn't that feel good? The truth is you're an extension of the most powerful energetic force in the universe—divine love and light. It's in your DNA. It's who you are.

I've witnessed a profound shift in many of my clients once they accept this truth. I once worked with a man who described himself as an "underachiever kid," born into a family of geniuses. Both of his parents were Ivy League graduates with master's degrees, and his siblings were straight-A students, and yet he barely squeaked through high school. After talking with him, I understood on a spiritual level that his poor performance wasn't a reflection of his brainpower. He was just as brilliant and capable as the rest of his family. The difference was that he had never applied himself, and over the years he'd convinced himself that he could only rise so high. And then one day, he fell for a brainy woman who inspired him to get his act together. In an attempt to win her over, he determined to show her how great he could actually be. Since he already knew on a deep level that it was within his DNA to be brilliant, once he put forth his best effort, he quickly achieved what he'd previously convinced himself was impossible— his professional performance rose to new heights, his confidence swelled, and he got the girl.

You, too, have it within you to be brilliant and achieve a great many things. It's your God-given birthright. I have a picture of myself as a baby in which I look nearly identical to my son Sam at the same age. I keep it in my office for when I need reminding of who and what *I* am. When I gaze into Sam's big blue eyes, I feel like I'm staring into a brilliant ball of love and light. His energy is magnetic; it lifts and lights up the room, and when I'm in his presence I have no doubt what this kid is made of—pure, unfiltered love and light. When I similarly gaze at the picture of my baby self, I understand that I'm made of the same stuff as Sam. I now look much older on the outside, but my insides haven't changed. I, too, am a brilliant ball of God's love and light. And so are you.

BEING LOVE

Knowing that at your core, you're an energetic extension of God's love is a profound truth and essential to your awakening. And yet there's a bit more to it. In addition to knowing that you are love, you must also *reside in love*. Residing in love means we must *be* love. What Spirit advises my clients and me on a day-to-day basis is that fulfilling our life's purpose hinges on making choices and taking actions that are loving and kind. Taking action is key. It's only when we act that we can effectively change the course of our lives in a significant way.

I recently took a car ride with a good friend of mine. She picked me up in front of my office, and when I jumped into the front seat, I couldn't believe the condition of her car. It was beyond messy—piles of garbage and fast-food containers, kids' toys jammed in between the seats, crumpled up papers and bags of who knows what on the floor. I had a hard time keeping my mouth shut. I wanted to say, "What the hell is going on here!" Except I understood exactly what was going on. My friend's car symbolized how she felt about and treated herself—with a lack of love and respect.

You cannot be love until you treat yourself with love. So

take a moment now and consider: *Am I treating myself with loving-kindness, compassion, and respect?* Look at how you care for yourself and your things. What's the state of your car, home, and office? How do you speak to yourself? Are you loving and kind? What about your body—do you take time and make the effort to exercise and eat well? Please understand I'm not talking about achieving perfection here. In relative terms, are you loving and respectful? Are you healthy? Only you can answer these questions honestly.

Sara, a Pilates instructor in culinary school learning how to master raw food cuisine, came to me for a reading hoping I'd be able to help her gain clarity around the strained relationship she had with her mother. As soon as I closed my eyes, raised my energy to the spirit level, and invited in Sara's deceased loved ones and spirit guides for insights, her grandmother came through with an urgent message for her granddaughter: Tell your mother to take care of her health before it's too late! Grandma impressed heaviness on my chest, which is my sign for unresolved emotional pain and the potential for a heart attack. I then clairvoyantly saw a nanny of mine who'd struggled with obesity. I said to Sara, "Spirit is telling me that your mother is overweight and will likely suffer from a heart attack if she doesn't start shedding some pounds." In my mind's eye, I clairvoyantly saw Sara standing above her mom, indicating that Sara was the older and wiser spirit. On a spiritual level, Sara was meant to guide her mother, specifically by embodying physical health. Upon hearing this, Sara confirmed that indeed her mother was overweight and on a physically destructive course. Grandma continued to impress me with feelings of self-hatred, doubt, and defeat. I told Sara that her mother's inability to love and respect herself was not only making her a very unhappy woman, but also sabotaging her spiritual and emotional progress and leading her toward a premature death. Grandma wanted her daughter to know that it wasn't yet her time, and if she chose, she had the power to change the current direction of her life. She urged her granddaughter to help her mother "wake up" and begin caring for herself. Not only would this save her life, but also it would help heal their mother-daughter relationship.

BEING LOVE MEANS TAKING CARE

The number one way in which I love and respect myself is by working out. The gym is my sanctuary where five days a week I'm able to physically and mentally detox, releasing any worries, concerns, frustrations, or stress I've got bottled up or that I'm projecting onto others. Once I take care of myself in this way, I'm in a better position to extend the love within me to those around me. My husband will agree: I'm a much nicer person after an hour at the gym. When I don't go—watch out! I can easily become irritable, snappy, and downright bratty. When I practice self-love and -care, everyone feels better, and this is exactly what I remind myself of if I start to feel guilty for taking an hour off for me-time.

I encourage you also to identify an activity that you can do regularly, if not daily, that makes you feel honored,

REAL TIME, REAL WORLD:

Taking Care

I was having a tough week of readings, so I meditated on what was getting in my way. I asked my intuition and my guides, *Why am I feeling stuck? Is the spirit world on strike this week or is it me?* Of course the answer was—*It's you.* It's tempting to want to blame someone or something outside yourself when things go wrong, but the truth is, if there's a problem in your life, you usually don't have to look much farther than the bathroom mirror to find the guilty party. Anyway, when I asked for clarity, I was clairvoyantly shown my diet. Specifically, I was shown a Starbucks coffee cup! My triple tall Americanos were hindering my ability to slow down, reflect, and tune in to my intuitive guidance. Take it from someone who's been there, starting your day with a heavy dose of caffeine may wake you up, but not in the "spiritual" way I'm teaching you to. When my body is running on caffeine, my energy gets stuck on the lower level. And when I'm on this level, I can easily become antsy and irritable, not at all the embodiment of love or divine guidance. By releasing bad physical habits and embracing healthier practices, like eating well and getting regular exercise, I become a generally more kind and loving person, not to mention a much more effective spiritual medium.

loved, and respected. Identify what feeds your spirit. What is it that makes you feel good? Maybe you're someone who needs a solid dose of sunlight every day. Or maybe you need quiet, reflective time indoors. Perhaps preparing healthy, organic food makes you feel cared for and loved. Or maybe all you need is a long hot bath at the end of the day to feel respected. Whatever it is, make time for it. Give yourself permission to take care of yourself and your needs. You deserve it. And so do the people around you. It's only when we love ourselves that we can genuinely and sustainably *reside in love.*

A client of mine named Suzanne weighed more than 270 pounds when I first met her. When I called in Spirit, her deceased mother came through and clairvoyantly showed me black spots all over her body, my sign for cancer that has metastasized. She then clairvoyantly imprinted in my mind's eye a half-circle and a U-turn sign. Along with the vision, I clairsentiently felt that Suzanne could avoid a similar fate if she "turned her life around." I asked Suzanne if her mother had died from cancer, and she confirmed that she had. I said, "Mom's saying you can have a different life than her, but you need to make some healthy changes." A year after our meeting, I received a hopeful note from Suzanne. She wrote, "I've totally turned my life around!" Since our reading, she'd lost 117 pounds after joining Weight Watchers and taking up running. She'd completed 5Ks, 10Ks, a 15K, half marathons, and was gearing up for the Chicago full marathon. She wrote, "I am a happy, healthy thirty-year-old . . . more confident than ever!"

FILL UP FIRST:

Angela's Story

When I was a little girl, I had recurring nightmares about my mother dying, and I would run to her room and crawl in bed with her afterward. She would cuddle me and say, "Don't worry, honey. I'm here." We had a relationship that I wish for all mothers and daughters to have, as it was a true blessing to be loved like that, and I know I'll never be loved that way in this lifetime ever again.

· The phone call I received from my dad on April 24, 2007, telling me my mom had passed unexpectedly sent me into shock, causing me to fall to my knees, screaming that I was going to kill myself. I wasn't prepared. I wasn't going to be able to handle this. Life could not go on without her. It just couldn't. My mom was an everyday angel, a caretaker, a giver, a loving and kind person who was entirely selfless. She was happy when she made others happy, and she lived life to the fullest each and every day of her life. She was my inspiration.

At the time of my phone reading with Rebecca, I had been struggling with my mom's passing for almost four years. Time does heal, but it hadn't done a thing for me yet. I'd had no closure. I hadn't been able to say good-bye to Mom.

I had no doubt in my mind that my mother came to me with Rebecca's help, and Mom went out of her way to make sure I knew it was her. She brought up things like the planter's wart on my foot (embarrassingly enough!), how I talk to her when I'm driving home from work alone in the car, and how I cut my hair too short last summer and bawled hysterically about it. I then started getting goose bumps up and down my arms, and as if Rebecca was sitting right in the room with me, she said, "You get chills quite a bit. That's your mom. That's her brushing up against you." My mom wanted me to know that she's proud of me, and that I've done a wonderful job stepping up and taking care of the family in her absence, but the most important thing she said was that I needed to focus on me now. She wanted me to start writing again, and use that creative outlet to make peace with her death and to nurture my own feelings and thoughts. I had given that up for a long time after she died and now I'm doing it again for both of us, but mainly for myself, just like she wanted.

AWAKEN DIVINE LOVE AND KINDNESS

In addition to going to the gym five days a week, I also carve out time every day to meditate, to quiet my mind and connect with my spirit within. Lately, I've been doing short meditative "blips" when I'm sitting at stoplights, waiting for the light to turn green. I take these little slivers of time to reaffirm that I'm an extension of God's love and light and, as such, I *am* love and deserving of love. In fact, the last time I did this, as soon as the light turned green, a car sped past me and cut right in front of me. How rude! Except, when I noticed the first three numbers on the license plate—628—I laughed out loud. That is my birthday, June 28, and I regard it as my "power sign." Every time I see it,

I know Spirit is making its presence known, confirming that I'm not alone. I'm surrounded and connected, an energetic extension of God.

You try it. The EnLighten Up meditation on the next page works to open up your heart, where the energy of loving-kindness resides.

In the Kabbalah tradition, the energy of loving-kindness centered in your heart is referred to as *chesed*. In Sanskrit, it is referred to as *metta*. The cultivation of loving-kindness, *mettā bhāvanā*, is a popular form of meditation in Buddhism. No matter what you call it, when the energy at your heart center is awakened, you can expect to feel love, compassion, empathy, and kindness flowing freely within you. A healthy and open heart allows us to love unconditionally ourselves, our children, our parents, and nearly everyone we bump into. According to the Universal Law of Unconditional Love, it is our true and divine nature to allow love to flow freely through us. That said, our hearts can often become blocked, and when they do, we may be incapable of feeling and extending love in a meaningful and authentic way. People with stuck or bottled up energy in the chest often come off as cold, selfish, and lacking in compassion toward others. Not only that, but also on a physical level an energetic block in the heart may result in such serious conditions as chest pain or heart attack. Sadly, I see this scenario play out *all the time*.

I read a man named Tony whose deceased father came through with heartfelt apologies for how he'd treated his son as a child. Tony confirmed for me that his dad had more or less ignored him, and he'd carried the weight of

ENLIGHTEN UP:

Open Your Heart

Close your eyes and take several deep breaths in through your nose and slowly exhaling out through your mouth. With each breath, focus on relaxing your entire body, from the top of your head down through your feet. Once you feel centered and grounded, imagine yourself as a magnificent tree, with your head reaching high into the sky and your feet rooted into the earth below.

Visualize a spark of emerald-green light beginning to glow in your heart center. Your heart sits within the center of the Tree of Life, perfectly balancing the weight of the branches above you and the trunk below you.

Continue to breathe.

With each inhalation, visualize this emerald-green light pumping your strong and steady heart. As it grows more and more intense, draw it in with each breath. Feel the light expand, loosen, open, and unblock your heart, *allowing for loving-kindness to freely flow.*

Breathe deeply and easily.

Set the intention to radiate the love and light within you.

Throughout the rest of your day, let your breath serve as a reminder that you're an extension of God and as such, divine love and kindness reside within you. If you forget or doubt this, repeat mentally or out loud: *Remove the blocks that stand in my way of expressing and receiving love. Help me reside in love always and in all ways.*

that pain, along with a fear of abandonment, into many of his adult relationships. In spirit, Tony's dad then asked me to reference his son's recent wake-up call and clairvoyantly showed me black spots around his heart, which is how Spirit symbolically communicates cancer to me, and I clairsentiently felt tightness in my chest. I asked Tony, "Have you recently battled with cancer?" and he told me he had. After a series of messages that I relayed back and forth between Tony and his deceased father, we uncovered the true cause of Tony's cancer—his childhood feelings of emotional abandonment had stayed lodged in his heart for years, only to manifest later down the road as stomach cancer that eventually spread into his chest. In spirit, Tony's father desperately wanted his son to know how proud he was of him and how much he truly loved him. Tony's father had come through to make things right and to clarify the significance of how Tony had chosen to live his life. Now on the other side, Dad recognized that his son had taken the more righteous path. Tony had become a devoted husband and father. He was loving and kind; he'd succeeded where his father had failed. Tony's father encouraged his son to release his childhood fear and pain and continue to be his innate loving self, as this would help him heal his heart and survive cancer. I'm happy to report that Tony has been cancer-free and in remission for three years.

With another client, a similar situation played out quite differently. A woman named Candace attended one of my group readings, where Spirit encouraged me to pass on to her a warning that her father should have his heart checked. I clairvoyantly saw black around his heart, indicating that he was holding on to some major unresolved emotional issues that needed to be released before they manifested in a serious and potentially life-threatening way.

As a spiritual medium, my role is to pass on messages from the deceased to the living; what the recipient does with this information is his or her own business. I'm just the messenger, so even when I've been asked to pass on a serious warning like the one I passed on to Candace, I know it's ultimately up to her how to use the information. I must stay out of it and be careful not to get emotionally involved. Experience has taught me the importance of remaining objective and simply stating the facts, understanding and trusting that any and all information that Spirit delivers is intentional. What I see, hear, know, and feel is meant to be passed on to empower and help my client in some way. If I start to empathize with a client during a reading, I run the risk of disconnecting from Spirit. Feelings like sadness, worry, and fear bring me right back down to a human level where my mind can often interfere with divine guidance.

A year and a half later, Candace e-mailed me to say that she'd never given her dad the message because "he seemed fine and was not likely to appreciate messages from the other side so we didn't push it." Candace then shared that since she attended the group reading, her father had had two open-heart surgeries. She wrote, "We can't help but wonder if it could have been prevented if we'd heeded [your] warning a year and a half ago." I was saddened to hear that Candace's father had struggled, but relieved that he'd survived. I speculated that because he hadn't resolved the emotional issues in a way that would have energetically cleared his heart, his doctors had to literally open him up and repair the damage physically.

AN OPEN HEART OPENS DOORS

Remember that much of your life—the people, circumstances, experiences, and situations—has shown up in response to your mental invitation, so as you begin to radiate and extend loving-kindness to others, negative influences will naturally fall away, and in their place, you will begin to attract positive encounters and relationships back *to you*. If you're a recreational yogi like me, you've probably said "*Namaste*" more times than you can count in yoga class, but do you actually know what it means? Most yoga instructors tend to say it at the conclusion of class, so I always thought it generally meant "Thanks for attending my yoga class. Peace out." Wrong. It's an ancient Sanskrit blessing that means "I respect the place in you that is of love, of truth, and of light. When you are in that place in you, and I am in that place in me, then we are one." Funny how it takes so many English words to communicate a single word in Sanskrit, but I digress. The point is that when you reside in love, you deepen your connection to those around you. Furthermore, when you express and extend loving-kindness, you naturally and more easily overcome life's difficult challenges. Did you get that? When you reside in love, you inevitably pass all those difficult tests you set up for yourself. You fulfill your contract. You fulfill your life's purpose!

I once did a phone reading for a married couple, Bill and Laurie. Unbeknownst to me, it was their intention to hear from Bill's parents in spirit, along with Laurie's father and grandmother. But as Spirit would have it, the reading started out very different from their expectations. Right away, I clairaudiently heard the name "Charlie" along with clairvoyantly seeing an image of Charlie Brown. I saw a spirit positioned above Laurie, indicating that he was a father figure. I asked, "Do either of you know who Charlie is? He feels like an uncle or father figure." Laurie gasped. She reluctantly acknowledged him as her uncle who'd died years ago. He felt heavy and serious to me, and emitted low light. But his intent was good. I felt his remorse and regret and claircognizantly knew that he wanted to sincerely apologize for something. I clairvoyantly saw him physically hurting Laurie. "Was he physically abusive to you?" I asked. She started to sob. Charlie showed me a school desk, which always means that a spirit is taking full responsibility for his or her actions in life. I could feel his realization that his abuse had scarred Laurie. He then showed me that he'd been an alcoholic and was now in a spiritual kind of AA on the other side, where he was working with his guides to understand where he'd gone wrong, whom he'd hurt and why. Charlie communicated that he'd mistreated others out of a lack of self-love and -respect. I clairsentiently felt that he wished he would have gotten this lesson while in life, but he showed me (again, the school desk) that he was now working on it in spirit. He asked Laurie to forgive him, not so much for his sake, but rather for her own. He cautioned that holding on to this distant painful memory was blocking her heart and holding her back in life.

After ten minutes of channeling his heavy spirit, I asked Laurie if it was okay if we moved on to others who wanted to come through; Charlie's energy was hard for me to continue to work with, as it felt so conflicted and dark. She quickly agreed, and admitted that before I called her for the reading, she'd mentally prayed that Charlie would *not* show up, as she had no interest in hearing from him. But as it turned out, as painful as it was for her to connect with him all over again, it was incredibly healing for Laurie.

Every spirit I read has its own unique energy. Some are light and bright, while others feel heavier, sometimes dark and more conflicted. The reason for this is that when we transition into spirit, we go to the place of our last thoughts, feelings, and intentions while in our physical body. Meaning, we pick up where we left off. So if at the time of your death your thoughts and feelings are dark—absent of love and light— when you cross over, your spirit becomes an energetic match. During the reading with Bill and Laurie, I could feel Charlie's dark and conflicted energy. It was dim, like a lightbulb with low wattage; it reflected his energy in life.

As a general rule, I don't work with dark spirits, unless they have good intention. I sensed right away that Charlie really wanted to evolve. He came through with a strong intention and desire to apologize and help lift the weight of his abusive memory off of his niece. In other words: He came through to *be love*.

PACKING LIGHT

Are you familiar with the saying "Love will set you free"? It's not only a popular bumper sticker and poetic song lyric, it's absolute truth. In his influential 1946 book, *Man's Search for Meaning*, Viktor Frankl wrote about his experience as an Auschwitz concentration camp inmate and finding a reason to live: "A thought transfixed me: for the first time in my life I saw the truth as it is set into song by so many poets, proclaimed as the final wisdom by so many thinkers. The truth—that love is the ultimate and the highest goal to which man can aspire. Then I grasped the meaning of the greatest secret that human poetry and human thought and belief have to impart: *The salvation of man is through love and in love.*"

Spirit has communicated to me that our lives are an exercise in love, and that when we find ways to infuse love and kindness into every challenge we're faced with, not only do we experience more joy and peace and a greater sense of freedom in our everyday lives, but also we become that much closer to God and to fulfilling our life's purpose. When we make the deliberate choice to extend love in our thoughts, words, and actions—in everything we do—when we choose to love in the face of our struggles and challenges, we finally understand why and what we've been put on this Earth to do.

A woman named Beth attended one of my group readings, where I was able to deliver messages of love from Jack, her husband, who'd committed suicide. Jack clairvoyantly showed me golf tees, golf balls, and a grave site. When I shared this imagery with Beth, she gasped. Jack had been an avid golfer in life, and every time she and her kids visited his grave they'd leave behind a golf tee and ball. After providing many more undeniable validations that her husband was present in spirit with her, Jack delivered this simple message: Find love again. Up until that point, Beth had been reluctant to move on. Her grief had been too heavy, and she was equally afraid of being hurt and abandoned again. Yet as soon as she received her late husband's blessing, she decided to be brave and take a chance. She began a daily practice of meditating and reciting affirmations that she hoped would open her heart and attract love to her. She repeated affirming words, like "As I move beyond past hurt and pain, I call in more love, and I know that I deserve love and accept it now, *and I am love.*"

Two months later, Beth e-mailed me and shared that she'd synchronistically met someone almost three years to the day of her husband's passing. She was surprised at the uncanny resemblance between the two of them (for starters, he was an avid golfer) and said, "I honestly believe my husband sent him to me." By trusting and residing in love, she'd found love again.

Residing in love can often feel like laboriously difficult work, especially if you struggle with low self-esteem or, like Beth, you've been hurt and betrayed and have painful memories of the past that have caused you to shut down and guard your heart. Any and all of these things can make us want to isolate and separate ourselves from other people. This is a very natural protection mechanism. And yet when we guard our heart so tightly, it's supremely hard to express love, not to mention receive it! So as scary or uncomfortable as it might feel, look for ways, however small and seemingly insignificant, to take steps toward love.

I was recently at Whole Foods shopping in the wholesale bin aisle where all the nuts and dried fruit are kept. All of a sudden I heard a loud crashing sound. I turned around to discover an older gentleman in a wheelchair who, in an attempt to scoop out a bag of almonds, had tipped the large plastic lid onto the floor, and with it about a pound of nuts. He was visibly shaken, embarrassed, and unable to clean up the mess on the floor. I watched as several people looked over at this man, none of them stepping in to help him. Except for one. A younger man stopped what he was doing and went directly over to the man in the wheelchair and started picking almonds up off the floor. From where I was standing, I could hear him make light of the situation, and both men started to laugh. The older gentleman started to relax, shaking off some of his embarrassment. I overheard the younger man offer to walk with him around the store and gather any other groceries he might need. While the older gentleman kindly declined the offer, the two men spent another five minutes chatting before they went off in different directions. Both men looked visibly lighter and brighter.

Readers, this is what it means to show up for others and extend love and kindness.

The action itself can be so very simple, and yet the effects are often significant. The poet Maya Angelou once said, "I've learned that people will forget what you said, people will forget what you did, but people will never forget how you made them feel."

CALLING FOR BACKUP

As you move forward in the days ahead, invite the Ascended Masters and the angelic realm into your life to help you awaken loving-kindness within you. Remember, you are not alone on the road. Higher guidance is available to you *at any and all times.* All you have to do is make the call and request a little roadside assistance.

PLACING THE CALL

Call on Ascended Masters like Jesus, the Blessed Mother Mary, Rachel, and Quan Yin, the deity of compassion, to get your love light flowing. As it is within the angelic realm, each Ascended Master has his or her area of expertise and life experience from which he or she likes to offer guidance and support. These healers and prophets turned enlightened spiritual beings are especially loving and kind, and when called upon, they can work wonders on helping you open your heart.

Mother Mary will occasionally visit me in my dreams. She appears with a radiant rose-colored glow around her. Her eyes emanate love and light. Her sweet smile lets me know she's shown up to support me. In general, Mother Mary's presence feels like a warm blanket, and she will often hold out her hand and take mine. Whenever Mother Mary appears, I clairsentiently feel as if my angels and guides want me to see myself reflected in her, and I understand on a deep level that within me resides the same

ASCENDED MASTERS

Ascended Masters, also called the "Masters" and "Lords of Peace," are powerful healers, teachers, and prophets who once lived on Earth and who have now graduated, or "ascended," to the higher spiritual realm. From where they sit now, they lovingly assist all of humanity (meaning, no matter what your faith, they're at your service). Their chief objective is to help raise human consciousness and balance out humanity's karma. A big undertaking, yes, and yet they volunteered for the job. These highly evolved and extremely loving spirits deserve our utmost gratitude and respect.

divine love and light that she bestows on those who call on her.

Another Ascended Master I work with is Sathya Sai Baba, the Indian guru and spiritual mystic who addressed his devotees as *premaswaroopa*, "embodiments of love." Sathya Sai Baba encouraged his followers to live in the awareness of the thought "I am God," and his message has been delivered to me in a number of synchronistic ways over the past couple of years, mainly by clients who, out of the blue, show up for readings with his picture or a blessed prayer scarf from him. Remember, it doesn't matter what religion you subscribe to; the Ascended Masters hear and answer all of our calls. They serve humanity. No ifs, ands, or buts about it.

In addition to calling on the Masters, you may also

consider giving a shout-out to Archangel Michael, whose name in Hebrew literally means "who is like God." This powerhouse angel is the messenger of love, mercy, generosity, and kindness. He's also associated with protection and is often depicted as standing to the right of the throne of God. In meditation, Archangel Michael almost always appears to my right, and cannot be easily missed. He appears as a broad, muscular man wearing a leather or bronze warrior outfit. He has blond hair, blue eyes and always carries a sword. I know—*hunka, hunka*. He looks like the Italian fashion model Fabio. Whenever I do readings, I call him in to help awaken loving-kindness within me and to give me courage in times of fear. Archangel Michael is very attentive. Almost immediately, I will feel his commanding presence inspire me to stand taller, reach higher, and shine my divine love and light on the world around me.

To feel the presence of Archangel Michael yourself, say aloud, or just think: *Archangel Michael, please be with me. Please help to protect me and remind me of my divine loving nature. Inspire me to make day-to-day decisions and take actions based in love, compassion, and kindness.*

reside: A RECAP

- In addition to knowing that you are love, you must also reside in love—meaning, you must *be* love. Make choices and take actions that are loving and kind. It's only through action that we can effectively change the course of our lives in a significant way.

- Expressing and extending loving-kindness outward starts from within. You cannot be love until you treat yourself with love, so ask yourself: *Am I treating myself with loving-kindness, compassion, and respect?*

- When you make the deliberate choice to treat yourself with loving-kindness and then extend love outward through your thoughts, words, and actions, your life will begin to flow easily and on purpose.

- In the ancient Kabbalah tradition, the divine expression of loving-kindness is referred to as *chesed,* and its energy resides in the heart. When *chesed* energy is awakened, you can expect to feel love, compassion, empathy, and kindness flowing freely within you. A healthy and open heart allows us to love others and ourselves unconditionally.

- As you continue to unblock your heart and awaken loving-kindness within you, call on the Ascended Masters and the angelic realm to help you. For a conduit of *chesed* energy, call on Archangel Michael to inspire you to take actions every day that express and extend God's love within you.

STEP 5

RELEASE AND REENERGIZE

If *feeling* love, *being* love, and *extending* loving-kindness doesn't feel easy, chances are pretty good that you've got a disruption in your energy flow. In other words, you're blocked. And until you're able to release whatever's in your way, be it an emotional block like past heartache or bitterness, a mental block like fear and regret, or a physical block like energy-draining people or self-sabotaging habits and addictions, you will find it nearly impossible to move forward with your life in a way that fulfills you and gives you a sense of meaning and purpose.

For this next step of your awakening, set the intention to spark your divine inner strength and courage so that you can release whatever's holding you back from a pure place of love. Once you release whatever's disrupting your flow, expect to feel lighter and brighter, as if your inner lightbulb got a bump from 75 to 125 watts.

Bob, a tall, slender man in his early fifties, came to see me for a private reading after he'd lost his daughter in a tragic car accident. Needless to say, he was distraught, heartbroken, and very angry. In our session together, it quickly became clear that his bitter and depressed energy was preventing him from connecting with his daughter's spirit. I felt her presence almost immediately, and as much as he wanted to feel her, too, he just couldn't let his guard down. I found him to be incredibly defensive and difficult to work with, and I imagine his daughter felt the same way. She kept providing me with information to serve as validations for her father that she was indeed in the room, but because Bob was fighting me on everything I said, I could not reunite them. The reading was not going well, until his daughter clairvoyantly urged me to mention "the black bracelet." I did, and *finally* Bob's energy shifted. He softened right before my eyes, took my hands, and began to sob. He pulled up his sleeve and revealed a black bracelet. He explained that it had been his daughter's. She'd worn it the day she died, and Bob had worn it every day since. Not only was this the proof he needed to believe his daughter's spirit was present with him, he confided in me that the physical act of wearing her bracelet had helped him to feel somehow connected to her every day since her passing.

I explained that there is such a thing called psychometry, by which a spiritual and energetic connection is made through inanimate objects. This is no joke or psychic fair hoax. Spirits have often confirmed for me that their energy is both retained in and drawn to objects and material that they wore or held often in life. In Bob's case, when wearing his daughter's bracelet, he felt not only remnants of her energy, but also a strong emotional longing to feel her, which invoked her spirit to be present with him.

Once Bob understood that his daughter was not really gone and that love doesn't end but only changes form, he was able to release much of his anger, pain, and despair. The dark, stuck energy just drained out of him. He left our session looking visibly lighter and brighter. In fact, he looked younger!

Over the years, I've continued to work with Bob to help him release any residual and lingering pain tied to his daughter's death. Where he was so resistant to Spirit at our first reading, he's now completely opened himself up to divine guidance. He's thanked me for helping "wake him up" and for "bringing him back to life." The pleasure is all mine. I'm grateful to Bob for allowing me to witness his amazing transformation.

HOW'S YOUR FLOW?

The great Buddha said, "Holding on to anger is like drinking poison and expecting the other person to die." Smart guy that Buddha, and in fact, his wisdom has been backed countless times by spirits who confirm for me that holding on to anger, or any negative emotion for that matter, is just like drinking poison and then suffering a slow, painful death. Daily, I connect with spirits who plead with me to tell their living loved ones to "clean up their act," "release," and "let go" of habits, people, and feelings that are not serving them, only standing in their way. They urge their loved ones to release any darkness they're holding on to before it either manifests as physical disease, follows them into the afterlife, or both.

I once did a reading in Omaha for a small group of women where a maternal spirit came through with a strong message for her living daughter, Jill: *Release your guilt and be free.* I clairvoyantly saw Jill's mother hovering above her in spirit, a pink ribbon, a large gathering of people, and a cluster of balloons, which is my sign for a big event or celebration. I said, "I'm trying to connect the dots here. I think your mom plans to be present with you at some future event that honors those who have struggled with cancer. Does that make sense?" Her daughter's face lit up. Jill confirmed that her mother had died more than twenty years ago of cancer and that she would soon be doing a sixty-mile, three-day walk for breast cancer in San Francisco. "Well," I said, "your mom is making it pretty clear that at some point during that walk, she'll make her presence known."

Fast-forward a few months later, and I received this validating letter. Read Jill's story below.

RELEASING DARKNESS:

Jill's Story

The walk was in San Francisco and I traveled there with five other friends. On the first day of the walk, we stopped for a lunch break and joined two other women on the beach who were also doing the walk. I sat down and introduced myself and started complaining about the San Francisco hills and how "I'm from flat Nebraska originally so this is not what I'm used to." The woman sitting right next to me said she was from Nebraska, too. Weird. She said she was from Blair. Even weirder. I said I only knew one girl from Blair. Her name was Katie Underwood and what do you know—she knew Katie, too. She said, "She lived down the road from me. Actually, my dad saved her and her friend's lives one night when they were in a car accident." I just stared at her in shock. I finally said, "I *am* that friend. Your dad saved *my* life. I've been looking for your parents for about five years now and haven't been able to find them. Ever since I had kids of my own I've realized what they did that night, bringing two bleeding teenagers into their house, was exceptionally kind and I wanted to thank them again."

She said, "I'm here honoring my mom who died years ago from breast cancer and my dad has since moved to Utah. You would never have found them. I was five years old that night. I remember when you came back after the accident to thank them for saving you. My dad always talked about you when he went over that hill on the gravel roads. He said, 'That girl beats herself up for that accident, but on these hills, it can happen so easily that if you hit a pothole, you're going to lose control of your car.' He always told me that he hoped you had forgiven yourself."

I hadn't, but now of course, my mom in spirit was telling me I had to. It was such a weight off my shoulders. I believe it was both of our mothers in spirit who brought us together that day on the beach to help me release my guilt and move on with my life.

This story gives me chill bumps. What I love most about it is that it's a perfect example of how often unbeknownst to us, Spirit is playing an active role in our lives, nudging us to let go of what no longer serves us so that we can get back on track to living our lives joyfully and peacefully on purpose. While Jill thought she was doing the Susan G. Komen Walk to honor her mom and also raise awareness of the breast cancer organization, in reality her mother's spirit was orchestrating the whole thing, inspiring her to do it for another reason entirely—to help her daughter forgive herself and bring closure to something she'd felt guilty about for years.

What's even crazier about this story is that no more than three weeks after I received Jill's letter, she called me with astonishing news—she'd just been diagnosed with breast cancer herself. My divine guidance told me she'd survive because she'd caught the disease just in time—and not because she'd received an early diagnosis but because she'd finally lifted years of guilt *off of her chest*. What Spirit communicated to me was that by forgiving herself for an accident she caused more than a decade ago, she'd halted the spread of a potentially life-threatening disease. I explained to Jill the Universal Law of Gestation: All things have a beginning and manifest into form as more energy is added to them. Said another way: Your thoughts are like seeds. Over time and with enough attention, they will take root and grow. In Jill's case, her long-term guilt had physically manifested as cancer in her chest. I told her, "You've been carrying this guilt in your heart for years, and your dis-ease has finally risen to the surface to be both emotionally and physically released."

WHAT STANDS IN YOUR WAY?

Before you can release what no longer serves you and only stands in your way of moving on with your life and experiencing purposeful fulfillment, you must be able to identify exactly *what it is*. Do you know what's got you stuck? In other words, when you think about it, what is blocking you from feeling love, being love, and extending love?

Not sure? I do nearly six hours of readings a day, and what comes up most often with my clients is some version of this: *I'm afraid.*

> I'm afraid I've mistreated others.
>
> I'm afraid I'll never love again.
>
> I'm afraid of being alone the rest of my life.
>
> I'm afraid to leave this unhappy marriage.
>
> I'm afraid I'll get hurt.
>
> I'm afraid I'll never get over my grief.
>
> I'm afraid I'm a bad parent.
>
> I'm afraid I'll always be broke.
>
> I'm afraid I'll never lose the weight.
>
> I'm afraid I'll never have the career of my dreams.
>
> I'm afraid I don't deserve to be happy.
>
> I'm afraid I'm not good enough.

The list of heartaches, frustrations, resentments, and unease that my clients express goes on and on and on, and what it all boils down to is *fear*. According to many spiritual teachings, there are only two fundamental emotions: love and fear. What is not an expression of love is an expression of fear. Buddha said that all of life is suffering. What he was referring to is the inner pain, stress, insecurity, and *fear* that we carry each day in our minds and hearts. Again, I have to agree with Buddha's wisdom, principally because it so closely reflects what Spirit confirms for me on a daily basis.

I read a woman named Ellen who was desperate to receive guidance around her husband's mental state. Peter was depressed, and financially struggling as well. Immediately her father came through in spirit and showed me that he was working with Peter from the other side to help lift him out of his depression. I felt her dad hovering around Peter and clairvoyantly saw them side by side, indicating a parallel situation. I also saw my father, Shelly, suggesting that Ellen's dad had committed suicide. I then clairaudiently heard him say that he wanted to help Peter "get it before it's too late." More than anything, I could clairsentiently feel a sincere and heartfelt eagerness in Ellen's father to help and teach what he had finally woken up to and understood. It made perfect sense to Ellen that her dad would be helping Peter—she prayed to him often to help her husband. After all, she said, "It takes one to know one."

Ellen's father communicated to me that Peter's real issue was not a chemical or mental imbalance. Nor was he suffering from financial ruin. Rather, he was trapped by plain old fear. I clairsentiently felt a wave of it come over me. This heaviness, like a feeling of being trapped or stuck, took my breath away. I got the sense that Peter's fear had consumed him to the point he'd created a self-fulfilling prophecy: He worried about money so much he'd manifested a money problem that triggered a deep depression. Dad communicated that Peter needed to take his focus off his money and instead focus on releasing his fear by redirecting his energy toward things that made him feel good. I clairvoyantly saw Peter hiking and finding feathers on the ground. I suggested to Ellen that Peter take daily long walks in nature and to be mindful of finding feathers. The feathers would serve as a sign from Ellen's dad that he was present with Peter, encouraging and supporting him. Ellen gasped at this suggestion. She revealed that Peter had a huge collection of feathers he'd found over the years hiking in "church," his nickname for nature. Finally Ellen's dad explained that when he killed himself he was in a paralyzing dark and fearful place, and it wasn't until he transitioned to the other side that his fear was released and he finally understood what divine love felt like. His work now was to help Peter experience freedom from fear while he was still in a physical body.

FACING FEAR

Just as darkness is the absence of light, fear is the absence of love. It follows then that if you're living in fear, you're not residing in love, which is the sole and *soul* purpose of each of our lives. John Lennon once said, "There are two basic motivating forces: fear and love. When we are afraid, we pull back from life. When we are in love, we open to all that life has to offer with passion, excitement and acceptance. We need to learn to love ourselves first, in all our glory and our imperfections. If we cannot love ourselves, we cannot fully open to our ability to love others or our potential to create. Evolution and all hopes for a better world rest in the fearlessness and open-hearted vision of people who embrace life." There it is—really, I couldn't say it better myself. In order to *feel* love, *be* love, and *extend* love, we must release our fears—whatever they are, big or small. We must allow our fears to surface so that they can be released. It's in doing this courageous inner work that we come to realize profound spiritual growth. Without a doubt, it takes a strong shot of bravery to face our fears and also to admit we're afraid in the first place, and yet most everyone you know has some amount of fear blocking his or her way, often called by a different name. Anger, resentment, frustration, heartache, and grief—almost every negative emotion you can think of is an *expression of fear.*

FACE IT, THEN NAME IT

Understand that if your life feels at all off or "ick," fear has likely taken control of the wheel. So the question is: How do you put love back into the driver's seat? First, you must have the clarity of mind to acknowledge fear's presence, and the best time to gain clarity where you haven't had it before is in the early morning hours when you haven't yet had a chance to pick up telepathic transmissions—that is, funky outside energy.

Before you get out of bed, I encourage you to ask yourself, *How do I feel today? Physically, do I feel loose and relaxed or uptight and tense? Mentally, what's going on in my head? Is it quiet and calm, or is my brain already racing with thoughts? Emotionally, do I feel at peace and content, or does something feel off?* As you lie in bed, take an honest inventory of how you feel and, as you do, realize that on any given day we each buy a ticket for a roller-coaster ride of emotions. Ups and downs are normal. What you want to identify is the presence of chronic fear.

Identifying fear can feel vulnerable and unsettling, which is why most people would rather ignore its presence. According to our couples counselor (hey, nearly every marriage can stand some work, mine included) it's when tension mounts, tempers flare, and things get really uncomfortable that many couples call it quits. They either throw in the towel on the relationship or never return to therapy. This is unfortunate, she says, because one more session would probably have produced the breakthrough results that would have saved the marriage. What I've come to realize is that it's usually when we feel most uncomfortable and inclined to run that we're on the verge of a major "aha" moment. So if you're reluctant to face your fear, I urge you to hang in there. Big-time release could be just up ahead.

While what specifically you're afraid of and where your fear stems from is interesting and introspective stuff, it's not necessarily important for this step of your awakening. The details—the *who, what, where, why,* and *how*—don't really matter. Simply identifying basic fear is enough. That said, if you want to dig deeper, consider reading my first book, *Spirited,* where I walk you through the process of identifying the root of your fear. Reflective work like this is valuable, and it takes time and your heartfelt commitment. It's a book in itself, which is why I wrote one!

AWAKEN INNER STRENGTH

To help you release your fears, even if you don't know exactly where or what they stem from, I want to share with you an effective little shortcut I discovered since writing *Spirited.* The following EnLighten Up meditation works to awaken divine strength in you, felt as a ripple of energy, a swell of inner strength to release any fear that stands in your way of embodying and radiating divine light and love.

Energetically, divine strength resides in the heart. In the Kabbalah tradition, this energy is referred to as *gevurah,* and when this energy is free and flowing, you can expect to feel a surge of strength that'll blow out any fear blocking your way. Conversely, when heart energy is blocked, it can often accumulate as anxiety and rage. You may feel stuck, unworthy, and afraid to take actions that would move you forward in life.

Just like you, I have my share of on and off days, and the truth is—from time to time I'll give an inaccurate reading. So when my husband, who is also my business manager, forwarded me an e-mail from a disgruntled client who said that while she enjoyed the experience of being part of a small and intimate group reading, she felt disappointed with the amount of information and guidance specifically for her. She said, "the reading was a big investment, something I was really excited about, and I was just hoping for an aha moment, validations for myself that would really make it feel real for me." I immediately wrote her back and agreed that her reading had paled in comparison

ENLIGHTEN UP:

Unblock Your Heart

Close your eyes and become aware of the rhythm of your breath. Let it slow down. As you slowly breathe in through your nose and exhale out through your mouth, imagine yourself as a magnificent tree, with your head reaching high into the sky and your feet rooted in the earth below.

Now refocus your attention on your heart, beating at the center of the Tree of Life. Imagine that whatever's blocking you is sitting heavy there. Continue to breathe.

Visualize the spark of emerald-green light within your heart center growing with brightness and intensity, awakening divine strength within you. As it grows more and more intense, feel the light melt away all fear-based energy that's blocking the flow of light throughout your body and standing in the way of you experiencing love more fully.

Breathe deeply and easily.

Set the intention to release your fears so you can freely and easily *feel, be,* and *extend* love. Mentally affirm: *I am willing to let go of all past thoughts and fears that are holding me back.* Throughout the rest of your day, let your breath serve as a reminder that you're an extension of God, and as such, divine strength resides within you. If you forget or doubt this, repeat mentally or out loud: *Strength and divine loving energy flows easily in, around, and throughout my body and life.*

to everyone else's. I offered to give her a refund or another reading. She thanked me for writing her back and gladly booked another reading. Situation handled.

Except that an hour later, fear got in my way. While I accepted that I'd given a less-than-amazing reading (I'm human, it happens), another part of me started obsessing. *Maybe I shouldn't do small group readings like this? Maybe I should stick to one-on-one sessions?* When I confessed my fears to Brian, he gave me a loving smile and suggested I go meditate. The guy knows me well.

I took five minutes to quiet my mind and meditate on opening my heart and releasing all fear-based energy clogging my flow, and I'm telling you, I really did feel a shift. I continued to remind myself throughout the day of my divine strength, and eventually my feelings of fear and inadequacy disappeared.

Eventually, through practice and repetition, as you continue to awaken your divine inner strength, you will naturally release any and all dark, fear-based energy from your energetic body. As an additional bonus, you may also discover that whatever's been blocking you is actually a gift, an opportunity for you to grow *even stronger.*

THE GIFT OF OPPORTUNITY

I recently ran across a TV interview on former major-league baseball player and manager Joe Torre. Now, this is a guy with a personal story about turning fear into strength and triumph. If you know anything about Joe

Torre, it's likely about his baseball wins—under Torre's management, the New York Yankees won ten American League East Division titles, six American League pennants, and four World Series titles. In the baseball world, this guy's a superstar. But what you might not know is that Joe Torre grew up in an abusive household where he was treated like garbage. His father was both physically and mentally abusive to his mother, his sister, and to Joe. As a result, Joe spent as much time out of the house as possible, and that's where he discovered baseball. The game became his refuge, a safe place to escape to when things got really ugly and scary at home. As fate would have it, Joe was a natural talent. He excelled at the sport. So much so that he was able to build a career out of it and eventually buy a ticket to a better life. Many years later and after much professional and financial success, Joe acknowledged his painful past and created the Safe At Home Foundation, with a mission of "educating to end the cycle of domestic violence and save lives."

As I learned this about Joe Torre, what rang loud and clear was that this is a man who signed up for, or "contracted," a father who would mentally and physically abuse him. Why? I believe this brave spirit agreed to this situation because it would allow him the opportunity to experience domestic violence firsthand, strongly motivating him to help others who similarly suffered abuse. Whether he's conscious of it or not, Joe's effort to help end domestic violence is spiritual work; it's part of his life's work. He turned his own personal tragedy into an occasion to *be love* and extend loving-kindness to others. What began as an obstacle became a divine opportunity.

The point of telling Joe's story is to say that whatever you're struggling with— fear of failure, alienation, heartbreak, inadequacy, or loss—and whether you contracted these feelings to show up in your life as a life lesson or created them through the power of your thoughts, understand that you have the power to release them and also grow stronger from the experience.

REENERGIZE

Once you acknowledge and release your fears, you open yourself up to receive, reside in, and *be* love. And while this is a wonderful thing, you're not completely out of the dark and scary woods yet. You must still be wary of anyone and anything radiating less than light and love. Bottom line: You must protect your energy. The best way I know of to do this is by becoming mindful of how you feel moment to moment, understanding what your limits are, and setting boundaries. When you know what you're willing and able to let in, it's easier to say no, and take it from me— saying no can feel *really good*.

As a spiritual medium, I'm particularly sensitive to what I allow into my energetic space. Not only do I have to set boundaries around the kinds of spirits I let in, but also I've had to create some pretty firm parameters between myself and the living. Because I sponge up energy nearly everywhere I go, I'm particularly wary of concerts, crowded malls, football stadiums, and amusement parks, where with that many people, I'm bound to rub up against some funky energy. In fact, as a general rule I don't even go to places like this because it takes approximately five minutes before my energy feels affronted by other people's "stuff" and as a result, I become cranky and moody and ruin it for whomever I'm with.

Knowing this about myself, when my son Jakob recently asked me to take him to an arts and music festival in downtown Denver, I hesitated. Crowds of people just aren't my thing, but he really, really wanted to go, so after a few minutes of pleading, I gave in and said yes. Then, just as I'd feared, as soon as we got there and fell in line with hundreds of people moving en masse, I regretted my decision. Dark energy was bumping into me left and right, and I quickly began to sweat, feel irritable, and get almost angry. I turned to my husband and said, "I have to get out of here." He gave me a look like "Really?" I shot one back like "Duh—this is the price you pay being married to me. I get weird in crowds." So Brian, who's an extrovert and loves people and big social scenes, played the hero and stayed with Jakob while I quickly retreated back to the house and submerged myself in a cleansing salt bath. *Ahhhh*—twenty minutes later and I'd released all the icky energy I'd sponged up.

Over the years, I've learned how to recognize what my limits are, and I know when to set boundaries and say no. Do you? Do you know what situations throw you off and bring you down? If you're not sure, take a look at the following list of factors and situations that can easily shift you out of a place of love and into fear:

· Gossiping, judging, or speaking ill of others
· Speaking ill about yourself

- Reading or watching news that focuses on hardship, conflict, and pain
- Not resting when your body is tired or not being physically active when your body has stored-up, unused energy
- Dwelling on past hurts or obsessing over the future
- Eating food and drinking substances that don't nourish you
- Working indoors for long stretches of time in air-conditioning, under fluorescent lights, and in front of a computer screen

Most of us do any number of these things from time to time, if not on a regular basis. Avoiding these situations altogether is near impossible. So instead of turning your life upside down or retreating to a cave in the mountains, simply develop an awareness of what habits and lifestyle choices don't serve you. Recognize how the situations and circumstances you regularly find yourself in affect you on a mental, emotional, and spiritual level. Learn your limits. The more aware you become of what your limits are, the more you can *direct* the energy around you, rather than react to it. Like my husband, you may be able to handle crowds just fine. Figure out who you are and understand that if something weakens, disempowers, and throws you into a fearful place, you get to set boundaries. Imagine that—you get to *choose* love over fear.

Still, that doesn't mean you won't encounter some of the dark stuff from time to time. The world's full of it, and you're bound to run into people here and there who really get under your skin and whose depressed and dimly lit energy threatens to block your energetic flow. Sometimes, believe it or not, people like this show up as helpful road signs, *pointing* you in the direction of a valuable life lesson. Just as you contracted specific lessons to learn ahead of time, you assembled a cast of characters to show up in your life to help and also test you. Often our most challenging relationships are our most powerful teachers. So if someone is really aggravating you, consider their higher purpose. What is he (or she) trying to teach you? Self-love? Humility? Patience?

That said, not everyone you encounter in life has a lesson for you. Sometimes, we simply bump up against psychic vampires or "energy vamps" who do nothing more than suck the light right out of us. You may encounter people like this in social and professional settings where you feel forced to interact with them whether you want to or not. And while you may not be able to avoid them, you do have the power to choose how you *react* to them.

I have a celebrity client I've worked with off and on over the years. During one of our regular phone readings, this client of mine suddenly began to act unusually nasty. She became very mad, throwing verbal daggers at the spirits and me for not telling her what she wanted to hear. I understood that she was going through a particularly terrible time in her life, exploited and hounded by the press. She was under a great deal of stress.

Still.

As I explained to her, the spirits that show up and the information and insights I'm provided with are completely out of my control. I'm just the messenger. For twenty minutes she let her guides and me have it. When I hung up the phone, I took a few deep breaths and resisted my temptation to go bitch about her to Brian. Instead, I listened to my intuitive wisdom and asked Spirit for guidance, and this is what I heard: *Her fear is a call for love. Send it.*

So I did. I spent the next ten minutes in reflective meditation and prayer, visually surrounding her with love, light, and compassion. When I was done, I put her out of my mind for the rest of the day. In effect, I released her energy. The very next morning, flowers arrived at my office with an apology note from my client. She realized she'd been completely out of line. It read, "Something shifted in me overnight and I woke up feeling peaceful, loving energy all around me. Thank you for being a light in my life."

Recognizing energy vamps and setting clear boundaries around relationships that undervalue and block you is the subject of another book entirely, but what I will tell you here is that you don't owe anyone your precious time or energy. If someone in your life is not serving you, you get to set boundaries to protect yourself, or as Gloria Gaynor sings, "Go on now go, walk out the door. Just turn around now 'cause you're not welcome anymore"!

My three favorite practices for protecting my energy in the face of someone sending and spreading negativity or fear are as follows: **Spread love:** Love is always more powerful than fear. To transform dark, fear-based energy, express and extend love. **Psychic shielding:** the mental act of visualizing a wall, pyramid, or bubble of protective white light around your body to guard against fear-based energy both physical and nonphysical. I do this every day as part of my morning routine. **Call for backup:** Ask the unseen world to watch over and protect your energy.

CALLING FOR BACKUP

Help is always available to us, even in our bleakest and most challenging moments, if we open our hearts to it. And when we do, we set miracles in motion. Call on the angelic realm and the Ascended Masters for protection against any external energy that does not serve you. Specifically request the presence of Ascended Masters like Ganesh, the elephant-headed Hindu deity who is widely worshipped as the "Remover of Obstacles." Each Ascended Master has an area of expertise in which he or she likes to work with us, and Ganesh is particularly effective at helping us remove fear-based blocks from our hearts and minds.

PLACING THE CALL

In addition to enlisting the help of Ascended Masters like Ganesh, consider calling on Archangel Gabriel, known as the messenger angel and the "strength of God." Gabriel will step in and do battle on your behalf against forces that you yourself feel unable to conquer, and cleanse your home and office space of any stuck or dark energy. In meditation, Gabriel appears to my left, often towering over me. He frequently carries a trumpet, and I know this means—*Listen up!* He often has important information and advice for me, always loving, and I feel hopeful after feeling his presence. I started calling on Archangel Gabriel more than ten years ago after having a vivid dream with him in it. I took this as a sign that he wanted to work with me. When I do readings, I call in Gabriel to stand at my left and offer strength and protection. I ask that he serve as a middleman, a kind of spiritual bouncer, keeping negative energy out and allowing spirits with good intentions in. He makes his presence known with a flash of silver sparkly light around the person I'm working with.

To call on Gabriel yourself, you may think or say aloud: *Archangel Gabriel, thank you for helping me to conquer any fear or opposing forces that may stand in my way. I welcome your strength and protection. Thank you for fully shielding me today from all darkness, negativity, and fear I may encounter. Please bounce all negativity off and away from me. Let my light transform all darkness back into love.*

Being a spiritual medium is all about managing my energy, because the nature of my job—speaking to people about heavy events and emotions—can be incredibly draining. For this reason I have to be cautious about allowing myself to become too rattled over things in my *own* life that may take away energy from my work. So when a good friend of mine and I had a knockdown, drag-out disagreement, I took steps to safeguard my energy.

I knew I'd have to see this girlfriend of mine again soon, at a party thrown by a mutual acquaintance. I had two choices: I could skip the party, or I could *ask for help*. The afternoon before the party, I took a few minutes to sit quietly and call for spiritual backup. During this short meditation, Archangel Gabriel made his presence known by appearing as flashes of silver light. I asked that my girlfriend only show up if it served the highest and best good for us both. If not (meaning, she was still upset and on the defensive), I asked Gabriel that she stay away, so that we could work things out when we were both better able to do so. I suddenly had a sense of clear knowing that she would not show up because of a last-minute change of heart. Sure enough, when I arrived at the party later that evening, the hostess said, "Just a few hours before the party, your friend called and said she couldn't make it." I smiled, knowing Archangel Gabriel was protecting me.

REAL TIME, REAL WORLD:

The Side Effects of an Awakened Life

Don't be surprised if in your new fearless and awakened life you experience a few unexpected side effects. As you're adjusting to a higher energetic and spiritual state, your physical body may undergo a "recalibration"—a woo-woo way of saying a period of releasing negative gunk from your system. As I've said before, everything starts energetically and over time manifests physically, so be prepared for the following:

DIZZINESS. I've experienced a lot of this over the years. I'd always attributed it to low blood pressure until my energy healer, Ariel, explained that my lightheadedness was directly related to purging old, junky energy out of my system.

TROUBLE SLEEPING. Your angels and guides like to work while you sleep, impressing you with wisdom, guidance, insights, and love—powerful stuff that may wake you up (which is actually the point!).

ALLERGIC REACTIONS. Don't be surprised if you become allergic to some foods you've always eaten. Because everything is made up of energy, including the foods we eat, as your energy is spiritually cleansed, it's likely your palate will need a bit of refining, too. You may become more sensitive to foods and substances that you once ate in abundance. I know it sounds kind of wacko, but this is exactly what happened to me. Within the last few years, I've become allergic to an odd combination of foods— salmon, garlic, cucumbers, and gluten. Thank you God— chocolate didn't make the list!

release: A RECAP

- If *feeling* love, *being* love, and *extending* loving-kindness doesn't feel easy, chances are pretty good that you've got a disruption in your energy flow. In other words, you're blocked.

- What's not an expression of love is an expression of fear. Once you acknowledge and release your fears, you open yourself up to receive, reside in, and *be* love.

- Take daily measures to protect your energy by understanding what your limits are and by setting boundaries. Be wary of anyone and anything radiating less than love.

- In the ancient Kabbalah tradition, the expression of divine strength is referred to as *gevurah,* and its energy resides in the heart. When *gevurah* energy is awakened, you can expect to feel a surge of strength that'll release any fear that stands in your way of embodying and radiating divine light and love.

- As you continue to unblock your heart and awaken divine strength within you, call on the Ascended Masters and the angelic realm for protection against any external energy that does not serve you. For a conduit of *gevurah* energy, call on Archangel Gabriel to step in and help you set healthy limits and boundaries around people and situations that threaten to darken and block your spiritual body.

REJOICE IN GRATITUDE

Once you clear your heart and mind of any conscious or unconscious negativity lurking around and release whatever fears have been blocking your way, you are free to receive an abundance of happiness, goodness, and fulfillment in your life. A client of mine who'd tried unsuccessfully for more than four years to get pregnant is a perfect example of this truth.

Claire had consulted all kinds of doctors and was seriously considering fertility treatment when she attended one of my *Spirited* group readings. At one point during the evening, I was able to provide enough Spirit validations to Claire to convince her of the presence of her "Gram," her father's mother, whom she hadn't seen since she was six years old. Gram clairvoyantly impressed me with an image of her rocking a baby, which is my sign for when a spirit is helping a child be born. I clairsentiently felt Gram's eagerness and excitement around this child's birth. I asked Claire if she was trying to have children and Claire enthusiastically answered yes. Gram assured me that Claire would be a mom. It was in her contract, and she should keep the faith. And what do you know? Within a week, Claire conceived a child. She followed up with this note:

> *In November of 2010, we were blessed with our precious Elliot. I credit my Gram a great deal for finally clearing my heart and relaxing my body enough to be open to getting pregnant. My anxiety and stress level proved to be a hindrance in the past. I often meditate and see my Gram smiling at me. I trusted in her and believed that I would be a mother, something I had given up on prior. . . . Elliot is the most wonderful gift that I have ever been given. Thank you for helping my dream to be a mother come true.*

To take the next step of your awakening, set the intention now to experience the fulfilling and purposeful life you're meant to have by sparking the divine light of gratitude within you. When you begin to live in a state of gratitude for what's shown up in your life, your day-to-day reality will take on a level of beauty you might not have noticed before. I call this creating Heaven on Earth.

A HEAVENLY LIFE

I've channeled thousands of spirits who assure me that our lives are meant to be joyful and beautiful—*heavenly*. What Spirit has communicated to me is that none of us have to wait until we physically die to experience heaven, because the reality is that heaven isn't *out there* or above you; it's within—meaning, the gates to heaven are open to you right now. What Spirit has shown me is that heaven is just a higher state of mind, and one we can ascend to in this life by simply appreciating what we have. It turns out that when we stop trying to control or resist the situations, circumstances, and people that have shown up in our lives and instead express gratitude for the beauty that surrounds us on a day-to-day basis, our lives suddenly take a turn toward *a whole lot better*. In the absence of resistance and fear, our lives begin to naturally open up and flow easily and harmoniously. Harmony is what heaven *feels* like.

Unfortunately, many of us fail to recognize what's beautiful about our lives even when it's staring us straight in the face! When I do readings for clients, and spirits clairvoyantly show me shackles and chains or a bird in a cage, I know that my client has created a living "hell" for him- or herself on Earth. Fear, grief, resentment, and bitterness are blocking the client's way, throwing him or her off track and off purpose. As a result, life feels like a death sentence.

I once read a woman named Susan who was holding on to deep heartache and resentment from a past relationship. As a result, she was almost impossible to work with;

she refused to let her anger go and was unreceptive to the spiritual guidance I was providing her. After nearly sixty difficult minutes together, she said, "I really don't see any way out of [this dark place] at this time." She had her mind set on what she wanted to hear and discounted anything else I told her. When the reading was over, we were both frustrated. More than anything, I felt badly that I hadn't successfully helped her. She was covered in anger and bitterness—a prisoner to herself. But then a month later, I received a very pleasant surprise in my inbox. Susan had had a breakthrough. Where before she'd seen no way to get out from under the emotional pain that had weighed her down for so many years, she'd finally discovered her own unique way to release and heal: Qigong. With roots in Chinese medicine, Qigong combines movement with breath and meditation to free up your chi, which literally translated means "intrinsic life energy." For my client, Qigong was just what the doctor ordered. It helped her release the fear and pain blocking her way, and as a result she'd finally woken up to her present life, one she realized she was actually grateful for.

In addition to the living, I simply cannot tell you how many spirits I've channeled over the years who express deep regret for not appreciating what they had when they had it. One of the more common sentiments I hear is "I'm sorry." Almost daily, I extend apologies to women from their deceased husbands who lament their failure to voice their love and appreciation of them when they were alive. Truly, I'm not making this up! While this might sound like a personal play to get a little extra admiration from my own husband (hint, hint) or stir up the war between the sexes, I assure you it's neither. Male spirits generally have a lot of regrets, and I think this has a lot to do with how many men are raised to suppress and hide their feelings and "man up!" It's often not until men die and cross over to the other side and are finally free to speak their truth that they readily express, and sometimes *gush*, love, compassion, appreciation, and gratitude.

Better late than never, I always say. As these spirits discover, gratitude transcends the physical world. In readings where a spirit expresses gratitude for a living loved one, I can actually see the energy of both the dead and the living grow visibly lighter and brighter. I clairvoyantly see what was dark and murky energy in and around the person's belly slowly start to brighten and flow. It turns out that gratitude works as a powerful energetic release. It flushes fear and darkness out of our bodies, so love and light can flood back in. In readings, it's not uncommon for me to see an energetic shift happen simultaneously between the living and the dead. It's quite beautiful, and in moments like what I'm describing, when I witness two worlds healing at the same time, I, too, feel a surge of gratitude for the transformative work I'm able to do in this lifetime.

THE ENERGY OF ALLOWING

Energetically, gratitude flushes mental and emotional blocks completely out of our system. It removes resistance, doubt, and fear and shifts your energy immediately up toward love and light, and when your energy is humming along and vibrating at this superhigh frequency, you're in the perfect position to manifest what you most desire in your life. The Universal Law of Vibration states that everything in the universe produces an energetic vibration, even our thoughts and feelings. Vibrations of the same frequency resonate with one another, which means that gratitude attracts its positive vibrational match—more in life to be thankful for. Robert A. Emmons and Michael E. McCullough of the Thank You Project report that "Grateful people report higher levels of positive emotions, life satisfaction, vitality, optimism and lower levels of depression and stress." When you live in a state of gratitude, your mind is fixed on the best, and therefore it will receive the best. Gratitude puts you into a state of allowing, where not only do you feel happier and more harmonious, but also you *attract* more feel-good situations, circumstances, and people into your life to feel grateful for. What you focus on expands, so when you put out to the universe through your thoughts, feelings, words, and actions that you're thankful, you attract more blessings and beauty into your life. Some people call this "receiving God's favor." Others refer to it as having an "abundant consciousness." Whatever you want to call it, I can confirm that gratitude will indeed dramatically shift your life and afterlife experience toward love and light.

◄O►

It was a Monday morning and I looked at my appointment calendar and realized I'd booked twelve solid days of readings in a row. I began to huff and puff. Truly, I felt like

I could blow my house down. I already had too much on my plate—kid stuff, marriage stuff, and friends complaining they never get to see me. My personal life was stretched beyond thin, and now this—I was looking at nearly two weeks of work without a break. I could feel the anger and resentment begin to rise within me. I went into a place of fear and I thought, *Rebecca, you better meditate* now *before your icky energy spins out of control.* So I did, and I pulled it together. I managed to get through the day without freaking out on my clients.

At five o'clock, I mentally put the CLOSED sign up on my forehead and made the drive home. By the time I walked through the front door, my fury from earlier that morning had made a vicious comeback. All over again, I felt overwhelmed and overbooked, and it didn't help hearing about Brian's leisurely lunch date with a buddy downtown, when all I'd had was a Luna bar! I swallowed my anger, made dinner for my boys, and then quietly retreated to my bedroom, where I could fume in private.

I don't make a habit of watching much TV, but that night I felt nudged to turn it on, and as soon as I did, I knew I'd been guided to do so. It was an economic story on *Dateline* about people who'd lost their jobs, their homes, and their sense of self-worth, and the desperate measures they were taking to rebuild their lives. Ironically, the two families they profiled were from Denver, so the story hit quite literally close to home. These were good families who'd once shopped for groceries at the supermarket, now forced to shop at the local food pantry; families who'd given generously to their kids at Christmas and were now only able to afford one gift from Goodwill. One woman had once held a top management position for a large company and now worked as a custodian and cleaning lady in the same building. Talk about being on the other side of the boardroom! I watched the entire segment, weeping from start to finish.

After it was over, I turned the TV off and spent several teary minutes in prayer, thanking God, my angels and guides, my deceased loved ones, my living loved ones, my clients, my friends—everyone I could think of—for blessing my life with such beauty and abundance. The next morning, I returned to work full of gratitude and had a fantastic week of readings. Not only was I crystal clear and able to make profound and solid connections between the living and the dead, but also my clients reflected my renewed sense of gratitude *back* to me. After one especially powerful reading that I squeezed in during my lunch hour, my client later sent me a handsome tip. "As a thank-you," she said, "for going out of your way." See what I mean? Gratitude acts like a magnet, attracting more blessings and beauty into your life.

The *Dateline* story was my wake-up call to be thankful for my family and friends, my clients, my divine gift—the beauty that is my life! If, as I did, you find yourself feeling down, caught in the middle of less-than-ideal circumstances, or if you're having a hard time seeing what's good about a situation you're in, a spark of gratitude might be just what you need to shift you into a lighter, brighter place. It's human nature to just go through the motions, day in and day out, but when we make a daily habit of recognizing all the beauty and blessings in our lives, our days take on more meaning and fulfillment, so to borrow from

Harry "Breaker" Harbord Morant, "Live every day as if it were going to be your last; for one day you're sure to be right."

AWAKEN GRATITUDE

To awaken the divine expression of gratitude within you, try the following EnLighten Up meditation designed to unblock any energy that's gotten stuck in your belly, energetically shifting your perspective from glass half-empty to glass spilling over. Trust me, when you feel it, you'll know.

Energetically, gratitude resides in the belly. In the Kabbalah tradition, this energy is called *tiferet,* and when it's unblocked, or awakened, you can expect to feel love, compassion, empathy, and gratitude flowing freely within you. A happy belly really does make a happy person. When I make a daily habit of meditating on the energy in my solar plexus, it usually takes *less than twenty-four hours* before I feel a noticeable lift in my mood and a surge of gratitude for everything in my life. No kidding, there have been times when after meditating like this for just *five minutes,* I feel so full of gratitude and compassion I feel like I could burst. I liken it to the same kind of crazy overwhelming joy and love I feel for my children.

Additionally, when your belly is open, your psychic abilities open up, too. When I meditate on awakening this center of my energetic body, prophetic dreams, premonitions, and psychic perceptions begin happening with intensity and greater frequency. This can be a good and a

ENLIGHTEN UP:

Soften Your Belly

Close your eyes and become aware of the rhythm of your breath. Take several deep abdominal breaths in through your nose and out through your mouth. With each breath, focus on relaxing your entire body, from the top of your head down through your feet. Imagine yourself in your favorite natural setting as a magnificent tree, roots grounded into the earth, head reaching high up to the sky. Take several more deep, relaxing breaths to firmly center and ground you in this natural space.

Once you feel centered and grounded, focus on your belly. Visualize a spark of golden yellow light beginning to warm up there. Your belly is the midpoint between your upper and lower body, the upper and lower root system of the Tree of Life. With each inhalation, imagine this golden yellow light filling up every inch of your belly. Feel the light expand, loosen, open, and unblock any stuck energy in your belly, so that the divine light of gratitude and beauty can flow freely through you.

Breathe deeply and easily.

Set the intention to awaken a depth of love and gratitude for everything and everyone you encounter. Throughout the rest of your day, let your breath serve as a reminder that you're an extension of God, and as such, divine beauty, compassion, and gratitude reside within you. If you forget or doubt this, repeat mentally or out loud: *I recognize the gifts in every situation, appreciating the opportunity to learn and grow.*

bad thing. Case in point: When I was on a work trip back in my hometown of Omaha, I met my mom for breakfast. She shared with me the details of her new career endeavor, and I could clairsentiently feel both her excitement and her tremendous fear surrounding the unknown. Later that evening, as I drove to a small group reading, I felt nervous and uneasy. I actually had butterflies in my stomach, which is unusual for me. My energy that night was distracted and unclear, and my ability to connect with Spirit suffered. While I was able to provide insights, they were generally vague.

The next day, I still felt fuzzy and felt a weird foreboding in my gut. I flew back home to Denver and booked a session with my energy healer right away. As soon as Ariel began to work with my energy, she nailed it. She said, "Have you recently been with someone who expressed fear and anxiety?" I told her I had. I recounted my lunch date with my mom. Ariel explained that because I'd gone into the lunch energetically "open," prepped, and ready to be a clear channel for Spirit later that night, I'd inadvertently sponged up all of my mom's stress. Her negative emotions had gotten stuck in *my* belly!

When the energy in your solar plexus is stuck or blocked, you may feel a similar sense of unease. You may also experience feelings of emptiness, loneliness, and disconnection between you and the world around you. Physically, you may carry extra weight around your middle. When I counsel clients who want to know how to overcome their struggle with weight, I suggest they stop thinking about the pounds and concentrate on what about their life they *do* feel good about. When you approach life with gratitude and focus on what's working versus what isn't, the extra weight, both emotionally and physically, is likely to come right off.

Eventually, through practice and repetition, as you awaken *tiferet,* the expression of divine gratitude within you, you'll be able to enjoy and feel thankful for your life, just as it is—both beautiful and flawed. There's this great Buddhist quote that sums up the life experience nicely: "Nothing's good; nothing's bad; everything just is." When you appreciate and feel grateful for whoever and whatever shows up in your life, you're that much closer to Heaven on Earth.

At this point, maybe you're thinking, *But not everything in my life feels worthy of my gratitude.* Amen! While there are days when I can easily relate to this sentiment, the truth is that when we're grateful and appreciate others and our lives, and trust that there's always a gift in every situation, the difficult and challenging times become a lot more manageable. Think of it this way: Gratitude is like having faith that everything and everyone that crosses our path has done so for a reason, either to help us heal or learn a life lesson, or as an occasion for us to *be* an expression and extension of God's love and light. Being grateful shifts us into an energetic state of allowing and receiving, and accepting that whatever life serves up is an opportunity for us to fulfill our life's purpose—to act generously, inspire one another, and let our love and brightest light shine forth. So be thankful for the difficult times, the challenges, and the mistakes. Within them is a divine opportunity to grow.

I once worked with a client named Jennifer, whose

daughter Mandy killed herself at the age of nineteen. They'd had a tumultuous mother-daughter relationship. Jennifer was critical of her daughter, put unrealistic expectations on her, and was often disappointed. Instead of focusing on what Mandy was getting right, she was quick to point out what she was getting wrong. Sensing that her mother's love was conditional, Mandy was rebellious and disrespectful.

When I met Jennifer, I could intuitively sense lingering guilt and pain. When I called in Spirit, her daughter came through right away. Mandy acknowledged her mother's hardness toward her. I clairvoyantly saw Joan Crawford as "Mommie Dearest." Jennifer broke down in tears. She said she should have behaved better, been a more loving parent, and appreciated her daughter. She blamed herself for her daughter's suicide, and the weight was heavy on her. Mandy clairsentiently impressed upon me her own sense of regret. I intuitively felt that she was acknowledging the role she'd played in her and her mother's strained relationship. It wasn't entirely her mother's fault, and Mandy wanted her mother to forgive herself and to "right the wrong" by turning her grief and pain into purpose. Mandy clairvoyantly showed me an image of her mother taking an active role in educating and empowering teens who might be in trouble. She did this by impressing upon me a flashback to my own high school gymnasium, listening to a woman speaker from MADD, Mothers Against Drunk Driving.

I ran into Jennifer several years later. She shared with me that she'd gotten involved with the American Foundation for Suicide Prevention and had started the very first chapter of the organization in her hometown. It had become one of the top grossing chapters in the country! Jennifer expressed heartfelt gratitude to me for connecting her with Mandy's spirit, and also for inspiring her to turn Mandy's tragic death into an occasion to grow.

◄o►

When a spirit clairvoyantly shows me an image of an eagle soaring over a mountaintop, a bird flying out of a cage, or a child running with abandon through a field, I know that spirit is finally free. That spirit recognizes his or her life for what it was—a series of opportunities to learn, grow, and spiritually evolve. With this greater God's eye perspective, spirits finally feel free to release their fears and cast aside the chains that held them back in life. Lighter and brighter, they float and twirl about, rejoicing in divine beauty and gratitude.

As I said earlier, you don't need to wait until you physically die to experience the kind of freedom I'm describing here. You can begin to feel it right now wherever you are by shifting your anger, resentment, heartache, grief, and fear into appreciation and gratitude for the people, situations, and circumstances of your life. Believe it or not, everything in your life has shown up with intention—to help you reach your divine purpose and potential.

A client named Collin got fired from his steady corporate job when the Detroit economy hit a record low, but instead of panicking and buying into fear, he took another approach—losing his job was God's way of "gifting" him with the opportunity to go out and create the job he really wanted to do. Within weeks, Collin took steps toward creating a new IT tech business that combined his love for computers with serving people who could learn from his expertise. Through word of mouth alone, his phone started to ring off the hook. After only six short months, his business was thriving. He'd doubled his previous income, was free to set his own hours, and even got to wear blue jeans to work—all because he'd chosen to see the opportunity and beauty in an unexpected situation.

CALLING FOR BACKUP

Granted, recognizing the beauty in difficult and challenging situations isn't always easy to do, so as you continue to work at awakening divine gratitude within you,

SPIRIT GUIDES

Unlike angels, spirit guides are enlightened spirits who lived multiple earthly lives—meaning, they were once human. As such, they have infinite knowledge, wisdom, experience, and applicable insight, which they now use to guide the living. Our guides come and go throughout our lifetimes depending on our level of need. At any given point, we may have a *council of guides* working with us to help us meet a particular challenge. Notice, I said help, not solve. Our guides can't take away our challenges, but they can offer us thoughts and feelings of comfort and clarity to best help us work our way through them.

call on the angelic realm and your spirit guides to support you. Remember, the unseen world watches and observes, and waits until we give them permission to illuminate our way.

Depending on where we are on the road of life, we each have at least one spirit guide working with us "on assignment" at all times. Sometimes, we have more. I've always had several guides helping me from the other side; collectively, I call my council of guides my "Master Crew." When I close my eyes and call on them, I clairvoyantly see them surround me in a semicircle. I have nine guides in my crew, three of whom I refer to as my "Master 3." My crew is on the ready, willing to step in and lend me a hand whatever the situation.

Our spirit guides are enlightened spirits who were once human and who are now between lifetimes. They've already lived multiple earthly lives, so they know a thing or two about the importance of gratitude. They have infinite wisdom and are extremely valuable in guiding us as we strive for a greater appreciation of our current lives and a greater understanding of where we're heading.

I've been calling on my crew for nearly fifteen years now to help guide me through various periods of transition and adjustment, and also to help me with day-to-day quandaries, like: *Should I have the uncomfortable conversation with my friend who keeps blowing me off and disrespecting my time or just let it go? Should I join my friends for an evening out or will it deplete my energy? Should I order dessert or will I regret it in the morning?* Really, I ask my guides for help *all the time.*

PLACING THE CALL

In addition to calling on your council of guides, consider calling on Archangel Raphael, known as the "Physician of God" and "God Heals." This angelic being of light is commonly referred to as a sage, a seer, and a healer. His energy provides physical and emotional healing by inspiring gratitude. In meditation, I often get the chills and feel a gentle breeze come over me when I call on Archangel Raphael. His energy feels nurturing and healing and, at the same time, amazingly powerful. He'll sometimes flash me the symbol of a caduceus, two snakes around a winged staff, which is my sign for healing.

On days when you're struggling to feel gratitude or recognize the beauty in a person, a situation, or the circumstances of your life, call on your council of guides and Archangel Raphael. Say aloud, or just think: *Angels and guides, thank you for being with me now, and for your help in opening my heart to freely give and receive love. May this opening serve to awaken gratitude within me, allowing me to fully appreciate and see the beauty in everything and everyone that shows up in my life.*

rejoice: A RECAP

- When you begin to live in a state of gratitude for what's shown up in your life, your day-to-day reality will take on a level of beauty you might not have noticed before, creating Heaven on Earth. Heaven isn't *out there* or above you; it's within.

- Gratitude works as a powerful energetic release. It removes resistance, doubt, and fear and shifts your energy immediately up toward love and light.

- What you focus on expands, so when you put out to the universe through your thoughts, feelings, words, and actions that you're thankful, you attract more blessings and beauty into your life.

- In the ancient Kabbalah tradition, the expression of divine gratitude is referred to as *tiferet,* and its energy resides in the belly. When *tiferet* energy is awakened, you can expect to feel compassion, empathy, and gratitude flowing freely within you. Eventually, through practice and repetition, you'll feel thankful for you life, just as it is—both beautiful and flawed.

- Recognizing the beauty in difficult and challenging situations isn't always easy to do. Call on the angelic realm and your spirit guides to support you. Ask Archangel Raphael, known as the "Physician of God" and "God Heals," to provide you with emotional healing by inspiring gratitude.

REST ASSURED

We can't always see the beauty and the gifts within our everyday struggles and challenges, yet when we look close enough, there truly is beauty and purpose—a divine plan. And when you believe that your life is unfolding accordingly, then you can relax and rest assured that *everything is going to be okay.* Time and time again, the unseen world assures me that we've each been given the opportunity to receive an abundance of peace, happiness, and fulfillment in our lives when we rest assured that there is a divine plan at work. So set the intention now to move forward with a victory mind-set, having faith and trust that your life is unfolding just the way it's meant to, by sparking the divine light of assertion within you.

This story perfectly illustrates how even when there appears to be no evidence to prove so, our lives are often perfectly on track. Oftentimes, what appear at first glance to be major hurdles and roadblocks that seem impossible

A PLAN AT WORK:

Lilly's Story

All I ever wanted in life was to be a mom. Twice my heart was broken. In 2004 I became pregnant. It was not planned. I'd spent four years in a relationship being abused sexually, physically, emotionally, and every other way. At the time, I was struggling to move on; I made the decision to terminate the pregnancy. At the last minute I tried to say stop, but the anesthesia knocked me out.

Five months later I was pregnant again, and this time I was overjoyed that God gave me another chance. I just knew it was a boy, and I had a name for him. Not long into my second trimester, I was rear-ended at 50 mph. Doctors confirmed that my baby's heart had stopped beating upon impact. I really felt like I didn't want to live.

That was when I met Rebecca, and my spirituality was confirmed that day. In a private reading, she said, "I see a car accident. Your grandmother in Spirit was with you. She is sad . . . about Andrew."

Tears streamed down my face. I told her, "I was in a car accident a few months ago. I lost my baby. Andrew was his name."

"He will come back to you in two years," Rebecca said.

I asked her if both babies were the same spirit, and she said yes. She also said my father, who'd committed suicide when I was eight, would be with my baby in spirit until he was born. I married the following year. After some health issues, my doctor put me on a fertility drug. There were complications, and two months later I collapsed and was rushed to the hospital. The next morning I awoke with my mother standing over me with a heartfelt look. "I'm sorry, honey. They had to take an ovary."

Now my dream to be a mother was truly shattered. I had no idea what I was supposed to do with my life. I was told by several doctors that I probably would never have children.

A year later, while finalizing my divorce, I began dating a man who'd also been told he couldn't have children. So, knowing each other's history, we didn't bother with protected sex. Two months later, I was pregnant. I still laugh about my doctor's reaction. He didn't believe me until he confirmed it himself. This was a joy I can't even describe today.

Nine months later, as I was about to deliver, my doctor told me the baby was too big—I needed to schedule a C-section. He suggested May 2. "Please any other day" is what I said. That was the date my father took his life. But in actuality, it turned out to be the best day. It was confirmation that my daddy had had my baby, gave him to me, and transformed what had been a day of mourning into a celebration of life. As predicted, I delivered almost two years to the day that Rebecca gave me that comforting message. She had also told me I would have a son, and I did. His name is Andrew.

to navigate turn out to be simply bumps along the road. As long as you trust that there is a plan at work and stay open—that is, in a state of allowing and being grateful for what's going right—the bumps in the road will eventually even out over time.

I've shared this amazing story about baby Andrew with many of my closest friends, and the majority of them have asked me, "If she was *meant* to have a child from the get-go, if it was part of her 'plan,' why did she have to go through such heartbreak and struggle to get there?" If you're similarly stumped, let me remind you that when life feels hard, you're either trying to control situations rather than allowing events in your life to naturally unfold, you've attracted difficult people and circumstances into your life by thinking negatively, or you've been presented with an important life lesson. In Lilly's case, she happened to have some big-time healing to do around her father's suicide, along with a few tough love lessons to learn about relationships before the timing was right for her to mother a child. The hard truth was that Lilly wasn't in a position to successfully love, respect, and teach a child before she first learned how to care for and honor herself. Remember, you cannot extend love if you're not *residing in love*. Once Lilly learned this important life lesson, baby Andrew came right along, serving as a spiritual pat on the back, a reward for finding the courage to heal, grow, and spiritually evolve.

A MASTER PLAN

Each of our struggles is the disguise of a divine opportunity for us to learn, grow, and spiritually evolve. While at times our lives may feel extremely challenging, our spirit knows what our mind forgets: There's a rhyme and a reason, a divine order to the chaos. I've had intensely vivid dreams in which I've traveled high up into the spiritual realm and wandered through a grand library—what I've come to understand are the Akashic Records, otherwise known as the "mind of God," or the "universal supercomputer," containing all human history and knowledge. In these recurring dreams, I leaf through a big book that's about three-quarters of the way written and land on a page that's been scribbled with a loose outline. Spirit has communicated to me that this outline represents where I am in my life today. Because I have free will, my story isn't all the way written; it's just an outline. The details have yet to be filled in by me. Ultimately, it's up to me how I decide to write my future. As it is for me, it's the same for you: Every day you make choices and decisions that either keep you moving forward according to plan or lead you astray. Thich Nhat Hanh, the Vietnamese Buddhist monk and author, reflects this sentiment well: "At any moment, you have a choice, that either leads you closer to your spirit or further away from it."

On an unconscious level, you have spiritual knowledge of what you signed up for, but on a conscious level your mind has forgotten the plan. And without a clear vision, a sense of the bigger picture, it's very easy to become skeptical and haunted by doubt and fear. If you don't believe

CAUSE AND EFFECT

I've communicated with countless spirits who express their regrets and frustrations over having failed to learn their lessons and follow their life plan. As a result, they have unfinished business, and two ways to go about it from the other side. One, they can offer support and guidance to someone who is still living and has similar lessons to learn; or two, they can reincarnate—that is, slip back into a body and return to the physical realm and tackle the same lessons again. Either way, they must finish their business. This is what it means to "balance out your karma."

Karma is a key concept in the Hindu, Jain, Buddhist, and Sikh religions, and it refers to our day-to-day thoughts, words, actions, and reactions. As I like to explain it, when someone has "good karma," that person is expressing and extending the divine love and light within him or her. That person's life is on track and on purpose.

I've heard karma referred to as a "cosmic tally book" where each of our actions has a cause and effect and where a negative must be balanced with a positive. Over the years, I've received Spirit validation of this principle. For example, I've connected with spirits who were greedy and selfish in life and who impress upon me that they must now make their actions "right" or suffer spiritual bankruptcy. This may mean guiding a living loved one to be more generous or reincarnating as someone who financially struggles and learns the value of gratitude.

While this cosmic concept of cause and effect is a little scary, it can be equally empowering. Karmic accountability means you have the power to choose who you want to be and how you want your life to unfold.

there's special significance to the people, situations, and events in your life, when something shows up that you don't like, you're likely to resist it. This is what it means to get in your own way, and unfortunately—resistance is our human nature!

And yet.

If we welcome life's struggles and challenges as opportunities to learn and grow, and have faith that everything is happening just as it was intended, our perception experiences a seismic shift, and suddenly we're able to see the beauty and gifts in every situation—the desirable and the undesirable. By embracing a new outlook and trusting that our lives are intentional, we can relax and feel more at peace and on purpose. We can rest assured.

A woman named Jan came to see me for a reading, and as soon as I called in Spirit for guidance, I was clairvoyantly shown a wheelchair. I asked her, "Who do you know in a wheelchair?" and Jan said that because of an illness she had to use a wheelchair at work. I was then claircognizantly inspired to ask her, "Do you think your life will be cut short for some reason?" Jan admitted that yes, she'd always thought she'd die a young woman. I continued, "Your deceased loved ones are waving you back. They're saying you have a long life ahead of you."

When someone has a lot more time to live, I clairvoyantly see a spirit take that person's hands and stretch them out as far as they can go, kind of like when you say to your kid, "I love you thhhhiiiiiiiiiiiiisss much." Jan explained that she had been diagnosed with rheumatoid arthritis at age seventeen and had had more than twenty surgeries since then. As anyone would who'd suffered that much physical pain and exhaustion, she was fairly convinced that her body was broken and it was only a matter of time before it completely went kaput. I told her that Spirit did not see it that way, to let go of her preconceived notions of how her life would play out, and to trust in divine timing. She accepted this information with a smile, but when she left my office, I wasn't sure if she really believed it. Later, she wrote me.

> Because of my illness I struggled with wondering what my life expectancy would be and what really the point of struggling every day to get to work was. I often made the comment at work that I didn't know why I was putting money into my retirement when I'd probably be dead before I got the chance to spend any of it. When I had bad days or particularly after another surgery I would wonder why I kept working.
>
> The messages you gave me really did change my life. The greatest change for me is that a weight has been lifted off of me and I feel like I can live my life because I don't feel like my future is going to be cut short. I make plans for the future now. I feel like I will know when I'm ready

to stop working and that isn't right now. I have two dogs now that I probably would not have gotten before because I wouldn't know who would care for them if I was gone. They have brought so much joy to my life . . . they have filled a place in my heart.

◄○►

Spirit has clairvoyantly shown me a roller coaster as a metaphor for life. Individual spirits often show me a set of roller-coaster tracks with my client's body sitting in the middle of them. Symbolically, the tracks to the left represent my client's past and the tracks to the right represent his or her potential future. When I clairvoyantly see a long ride of ups and downs to the left of my client, I know that person has struggled significantly in the past. In particularly clear readings, I may also be provided with a claircognizant sense of how long my client has been struggling. If I clairvoyantly see just a few bumps to the right, followed by a smooth ride up ahead, then I know that person has only a few more lessons to learn before his or her life will ease up and flow freely and on purpose. Spirit will sometimes impress me with an actual date for when a client's roller-coaster ride will come to a full stop. However bumpy or smooth, spirits urge me to pass on to their living loved ones that the often dramatic ups and downs, the twists and turns, and the sometimes unsettling ride of life are only temporary. Furthermore, they reassure me, we've each only bought a ticket for the ride we can stomach. In the later years of his life, my father,

Shelly, gave me a ring inscribed with "*Gam Ze Ya A'vor.*" It means in Hebrew "This too shall pass." I wear it when I need a shot of courage and a physical reminder that our lives are temporary and ever changing. The Universal Law of Rhythm reminds us that change is constant. Life goes up and down; it swings low and high. It's constantly correcting and changing course.

DEVIATING FROM THE PLAN

Okay, so life is a series of ups and downs, a roller coaster, and some people sign up for a wild ride, but maybe you're still left wondering about the really upsetting stuff, such as random and horrifying events like the slaughter in Aurora, Colorado, in 2012, when a gunman in a gas mask and body armor killed twelve people at a midnight premiere of a Batman movie, or the devastating heartbreak that comes with unexpectedly losing a child, as so many parents experienced that same year in Newtown, Connecticut. Why would anyone sign up for that?

Unarguably, this is tough one and begs the question—*Why?* No doubt, tragic events are very difficult to rationalize, and my thoughts, prayers, love, and light go out to those who've lost loved ones in this way. That said, I hope you can find some comfort in what I say next. What Spirit has communicated to me countless times is that all of us sign up for experiences and circumstances to unfold in our lifetimes that will allow for our greatest spiritual growth, and sometimes this means certain spirits volunteer to "take one for the team," in order to touch the lives of those around them and oftentimes teach, guide, and inspire the greater community to make significant and meaningful change. Understand that in most cases, these volunteers are spiritually way ahead of us. They've been here before—many times—and have already passed many of their own life lessons, and because of this they can afford to sacrifice *this life* for the express purpose of serving others. Understand, too, that selfless service is one of the highest expressions of God's divine love, and so by having the courage and willingness to extend themselves in this way, these people further brighten and lighten their own spirit.

Spirits have relayed that from a human perspective it's often unthinkable that anyone would assist in unfortunate and needless tragedies. But from a spiritual perspective, a sacrifice like this is considered an empowering experience, in which the spirit is enriched and the physical life is only temporarily affected. Time and time again, spirits have provided me with this same consistent understanding of why bad things happen to good people, and they're excited to share this discovery with the living in hopes that it will help assuage our grief. Spirits have clairvoyantly shown me a coloring book, indicating that once on the other side, they've finally "connected the dots" and gained an understanding of the bigger picture. Tragedy, they communicate, is often not what it seems. Events are neither good nor bad, fair nor unjust. Labels and determinations like this are creations of the mind. Human error.

Through spiritual insights gained in readings and deep meditation, what I've come to understand is that in the case of a sudden or "tragic" death, as in a car accident or a murder, the spirit will easily and effortlessly eject and disassociate from the body and begin the ascent back home. The spirit will quickly rise out of the body, typically leaving from one of two places: up through the crown or out through the "soul center," the space between the heart and the throat. Some spirits are met by their angels and guides to help them cross over, while more advanced and enlightened spirits know exactly where to go and what to do. As soon as they eject, they're on their way. Other spirits will choose to remain near the scene of their physical death for a brief period of time to comfort their living loved ones, typically ascending within forty-eight hours.

I once had a vividly powerful dream where I was witnessing a person die in a horrific car accident. I watched as the spirit left the body, like a big bubble of bright light floating up and out of the body. I then clairaudiently heard someone explain that there was no point for this spirit to physically suffer because there was no lesson in that. A few days later, I did a reading for a woman who had recently lost her husband in a car accident that was remarkable in its resemblance to the scene I'd witnessed in my dream. In fact, as I read the woman, my dream flashed back in my mind, and this was my validation that it had been her husband who'd narrated my dream and clairvoyantly shown me his death, so that I could pass on assurance to his wife that he did not suffer. He'd felt no pain and he was now in "a brighter place."

In the case of the grizzly Aurora shooting, which happened less than five miles from my own home, there appears to be only one way to look at this painful and shocking event—it should never have happened. To listen to my husband try and explain this horrendous act of darkness to our boys was both sad and painful. He told them that this young man committed an evil act, hurting and killing many innocent people. He explained that there are some people in the world who become disconnected from God and do bad things. I then added, "And while we might be tempted to live in fear that this could happen anywhere, anytime, to anyone, we should instead focus our energy on love, by sending our thoughts and prayers to the victims and their families."

And yet as senseless as this event seems to be—from a spiritual perspective, that is—seen through God's eyes, the Aurora shooting was a slight deviation but still part of a bigger plan. This may be difficult to hear and even harder to accept, but what Spirit has shown me is that we're all born with a few predetermined "exit points," departure dates when our physical lives will end. What we may call an accident or a tragedy is often God's way of summoning a spirit back home after a person has fulfilled what his or her spirit came to Earth to do. On an unconscious level, no spirit leaves the body without its consent. Considering this, it's not only possible, but also very likely, that the victims of the Aurora shooting agreed prior to being born to come together at that exact place and time to volunteer their lives as a means to unite a community, and also inspire individual lessons in forgiveness. Understand that every death has the potential to create a profound transformation for the living, provided that those left behind choose to learn from the experience and allow it to shift their own energy up toward love and light.

In the aftermath of the Aurora shooting, I witnessed my own community come together and lighten and brighten. Some of my friends and neighbors were just a few of the many who willingly jumped in to help out the families of the victims, either with financial contributions or by volunteering their time and energy facilitating support groups and offering individual counseling. This sad event gave many people an opportunity to shine.

CHOOSING A DARK ROAD

So now that you understand that some spirits selflessly "take one for the team" to encourage individual and collective spiritual growth, what about the bad guys—those who commit selfish, violent acts? How do their crimes and offenses fit into the bigger picture? What Spirit has shown me is that there are unfortunate instances when an individual can become so lost and disconnected from his or her love, that he (or she) becomes engulfed in darkness. In this dark and lonely place, and armed with the power of free will, abusive acts are not entirely uncommon.

This is the exception and not the rule.

Nearly every act, circumstance, and event has a divine purpose. What I've learned from Spirit is that sometimes a person will choose to play a dark role in life to accomplish a "team" goal. Their darkness inspires an inverse effect—individual and collective shifts up toward love and light. In this respect, what at first appears to be "tragic" turns out to be a blessing in disguise.

During a reading with a female client, Spirit clairvoyantly showed me two very different stories. Like movies playing out in my mind's eye, I clairvoyantly saw that she was currently the victim in an abusive relationship and that she had been the abuser in a past life. (Insights into past lives aren't necessarily my thing, but I'm occasionally provided with this kind of information when it will shine a spotlight on a troubling situation.) On a spiritual level, by playing the role of both the abuser and abused, my client was balancing her karmic debt. The kind of role reversal I'm describing here may sound crazy. Who, in their right mind, would sign up for something like this? No one! But remember, the mind forgets what the spirit remembers: Our current lives are fleeting and temporary, and so we sign up for the experiences that will provide us with the most powerful and profound opportunities to grow and evolve.

Every event, even the tragic and heartbreaking, has a rhyme and a reason. Spirit urges us to believe, trust, and rest assured that there's a greater plan at work, providing each one of us with opportunities to grow. Viktor Frankl wrote in *Man's Search for Meaning*, "The way in which a man accepts his fate and all the suffering it entails, the way in which he takes up his cross, gives him ample opportunity—even under the most difficult circumstances—to add a deeper meaning to his life."

Do you know the story of the Coble family tragedy and miracle? This is the story of Chris and Lori Coble, who lost all three of their children in an automobile accident when a big rig slammed into the back of their minivan. After the Cobles buried Kyle (five), Emma (four), and Katie (two), they suffered from deep and devastating grief, each making a pact not to commit suicide and leave the other one alone. Three months after the accident, they decided to give life another chance. They began in vitro fertilization treatments in an effort to get pregnant. As fate would have it, Lori soon became pregnant with triplets—two girls and a boy. Almost a year to the date of losing their beloved Kyle, Emma, and Katie, the Cobles welcomed three new babies into the world. When we look at this story through God's eyes, it's a perfect illustration of divine orchestration. A tragedy transformed into a miracle.

I have worked with countless parents who have lost young children, and in my opinion, this is the greatest loss one can experience. And yet again, what Spirit has shown me is that many selfless spirits *choose* to incarnate to help the people around them learn something very specific, such as the importance of letting go and forgiving, or to assist them in finding their faith and connection to God. Once their mission is complete, they return back home to the spiritual realm. This is often the case with the death of a child.

During a reading with his mother and sister, the loving spirit of a young man named Kevin Hersh came through to assure them that his early death was intentional. He'd signed up to be of service to others and exit early. On a conscious mind level he had no clue he was going to die young, but on a spirit level he did, and his life unfolded exactly as planned. He'd died a hero by rescuing a drowning girl in the ocean. In the act of saving someone else, he'd sacrificed his own life. He died the same way he lived, by being an example of what it looks like to extend love and light, and he urged his mother and sister to find closure around

SELFLESS SACRIFICE:

Elaine's Story

"I see Kevin and he's holding a Hershey Kiss. Does he like chocolate?"

I was sitting on a sofa in Rebecca Rosen's cozy office and these were the first words she said to me. My son, Kevin, had died just a month ago and two of my friends who are social workers had insisted that I see Rebecca. In fact, they called to facilitate an early appointment for me.

I knew why Kevin was holding a Hershey Kiss. Yes, he did like chocolate, but the Hershey Kiss was to let me know that it was indeed him. Hershey Kisses are like a symbol for our family, our last name being Hersh. I serve Hershey Kisses at home, and when I taught, I always handed out Hershey Kisses [to students].

Then Rebecca said that he was showing a Superman shirt. "He's saying that he is proud. He knows he is a hero and he could not have done anything different," said Rebecca. Kevin did save a life, but, sadly, in the process he lost his. Kevin was one who did so many things to help make the world a better place, and saving a life was the ultimate.

Rebecca went on to say she felt a pressure in her chest. "Did Kevin drown?" she asked. "Yes, he did," I told her, "after saving someone in Cozumel, Mexico, who was caught in an undertow and had been pulled far away from shore." Kevin wanted me to know that he was fine. What a wonderful feeling for me to realize I really didn't lose my son, he is just around the corner....

I find comfort in knowing my loved ones are still a part of my life. They do survive, but in a different form. They are always around and watching over us with love. I hope that other bereaved people … realize that death is not an end. It is also a beginning to a different kind of life.

his death and enjoy life. He wanted his mother, who also lost her husband three years after losing Kevin, to understand and know that there is indeed an afterlife and that eventually they would all meet up again.

EARTH ANGELS

Children who die what appear to be unnatural deaths—in pregnancy, infanthood, childhood, and early adulthood—are often spirits on assignment from the spiritual realm. These children are enlightened beings of light; despite their age, they're highly evolved. As I've come to understand it, these Earth angels (also called "indigo" or "crystal" children) tend to reside on Earth for a short period of time, spreading love and light and sharing their often remarkable gifts with all those they come into contact with.

I have a regular client named Anne whose precious eight-year-old son, Jacob, has a brain tumor, and every time I see her she asks the same question, "Why, why, why?" And while it's been hard for her to hear, the answer I get from Spirit is always the same: Jacob chose this.

The first time I passed on what Spirit was telling me—that Jacob had signed up to have brain cancer to help advance medicine—Anne's mouth fell on the floor. She wasn't angry with me for saying the unthinkable. Rather, she confirmed that Jacob's rare condition was constantly being tested and evaluated, which had led to research trials that his doctors felt confident would provide them with a scientific breakthrough.

Every time I see Anne, she recounts with amazement how selfless and resilient her little guy continues to be. While his buddies are outdoors playing and living normal lives, he's lying in a hospital bed and seems "happy as can be." During our most recent reading, I was guided by Spirit to pass on the following words on Jacob's behalf: *Don't pity me. Celebrate and learn from me.*

Another such Earth angel you may even be familiar with is Mattie J. T. Stepanek, the little boy Oprah frequently had on her daytime talk show, who wrote inspired poetry he called *heartsongs*. Mattie was severely handicapped, battling a rare form of muscular dystrophy that eventually took his life before he reached his fourteenth birthday. During his short time on Earth, Mattie inspired millions, extending hope and healing to people all over the world.

The unseen world has literally shown me a line out the door of older, spiritually advanced and evolved spirits waiting to be born with handicaps and illnesses. Because these spirits know a physical life is only temporary, they're willing to endure the short-term discomfort and pain for our benefit. They voluntarily choose to be born into what we consider broken bodies to extend their love and light. It's natural to feel some amount of sorrow and sympathy for the sick and disabled, but what they really deserve is our highest respect. These brave and selfless spirits are our greatest teachers, and it's our responsibility to honor and learn from them.

I consider myself blessed that because of the work I do, I get the opportunity to meet remarkable spirits like Mattie J. T. Stepanek. Their loving and kind energy lights me up! When they come through in readings, it's as if I've just taken a shot of espresso. My head starts to buzz and my own energy lifts. Oftentimes, I have to talk a million miles per minute just to keep up with their lightning-fast energy. It's a wonderfully exhilarating feeling.

AWAKEN TRUST

While it may be hard to understand and accept tragic and shocking deaths, or any event or circumstance in your life that feels off or plain old wrong, in the struggle to make sense of it all, I encourage you to pray for faith and assurance that your life is unfolding according to plan. I often encourage my clients to "pray big," to ask to see things with a broader perspective. The philosopher and theologian Søren Kierkegaard said, "The function of prayer is not to influence God, but rather to change the nature of the one who prays." In other words, pray for a shift within you. Pray for a change in perception, a switch from skepticism to trust, and when you do, you'll likely discover you're able to move past your grief, heartache, frustration, fear, and resistance with a greater sense of ease.

I read a woman named Naomi whose guides clairvoyantly showed me that her husband was sick and she was thinking of leaving him. I clairvoyantly saw a man lying in bed and Naomi standing at his side caring for him, and I clairsentiently felt her unhappiness, along with a feeling of being trapped, smothered by his low, heavy energy. I could feel her desire to run away. Naomi confirmed that her marriage had been rocky for a while. She'd thought about divorce, but her husband had been recently diagnosed with cancer and she felt guilty even considering that now. I was then clairvoyantly shown an image of Naomi with her feet cemented to the ground, her energy lightening and brightening the space around her husband's bed, like a lightbulb being turned on. I told her, "Your guides are showing me that if you fill yourself up with love and light and extend this to your husband, you can be free without leaving. They're impressing upon me that despite your being frustrated and worn down by your situation, it's helping you to grow." I then saw that eventually she would shed her current circumstances and find new reasons to be happy. I was clairvoyantly shown a snakeskin, representing Naomi's spiritual growth and transformation. I told her to be on the lookout for snakes, as this would be a sign from Spirit that her life was unfolding according to plan and to have courage and faith that she was on the right path. Just hours after our reading, Naomi e-mailed me with an astounding validation. She was taking her dog for a walk, when suddenly he stopped in his tracks. She looked down at the ground and spotted a recently shed snakeskin under a pile of rocks. Truly, I'm not making this up! The signs from Spirit are everywhere as soon as you take the time to look for them.

AWAKEN DIVINE FAITH AND TRUST

To help awaken divine faith, trust, and assurance within you, close your eyes and spend five quiet minutes in meditation. The following EnLighten Up meditation is designed to unblock any energy that's gotten stuck in your pelvis, specifically in your right hip, so that you can move forward with assertion and faith that your life is unfolding according to plan.

Energetically, divine trust and assertion resides in the sacral center, specifically the right hip. In the Kabbalah tradition, this energy is called *netzach,* and when it's unblocked, or awakened, you can expect to feel a sense of determination, assertion, and personal conviction flowing freely within you. Healthy *netzach* energy provides you with a sense of personal power in the world, which makes you feel grounded and secure, comfortable with where you fit into the big scheme of things. Conversely, when *netzach* energy is blocked, you're likely to feel overwhelmed, insecure, powerless, and basically beaten down by life. Physically, you may suffer impotence; uterine, bladder, or kidney trouble; or chronic low back pain.

Eventually, as through practice and repetition you awaken the expression of divine trust within you, when small hiccups or larger and more challenging situations surface, they won't unhinge you. You'll be able to stay centered, faithful, and assured that there's a gift or a valuable lesson to be learned, and you'll work through it. Furthermore, when you face your challenges head-on, with the intent to move past them, you'll inevitably resolve them.

ENLIGHTEN UP:

Loosen Your Hips

Close your eyes and take several deep breaths in through your nose and out through your mouth. With each breath, focus on relaxing your entire body, from the top of your head down through your feet. Imagine yourself out in nature as a magnificent tree, feet firmly rooted in the earth and your head reaching high into the sky. Take several more deep, relaxing breaths to firmly center and ground you in this natural space.

Once you feel centered and grounded, focus your attention on your sacral center, the space between your hips.

Continue to breathe.

Now visualize a spark of amber-orange light beginning to glow in your right hip pocket. Imagine this spark of amber-orange light located within the extensive root system of the Tree of Life. With each inhalation, imagine this amber-orange light filling up every inch of your right hip. Feel the light expand, loosen, open, and unblock any stuck energy there, so that the divine light of faith, trust, assurance, and assertion can flow freely through your energetic body.

Breathe deeply and easily.

Set the intention to free your conscious and unconscious mind of any fears, skepticism, and doubt. Throughout the rest of your day, let your breath serve as a reminder that you're an extension of God, and as such, divine faith and trust resides within you. If you forget or doubt this, repeat mentally or out loud: *My faith and knowing is restored that all the events in my life are unfolding in divine timing and order, according to God's will.*

A good friend of mine discovered that her husband of twenty-plus years was cheating on her. As anyone would be, she was heartbroken. After several weeks of slumping around in victim mode, she asked for a divorce and determined to re-create her life. She decided that staying in the same town as her ex-husband and his soon-to-be new wife would be too difficult (not to mention, maddening!) and would likely stall her movement forward, so she packed up and moved from Ohio across country to Denver. Making a fresh start in a new state, she said, was not easy. Initially she felt lost, alone, and uncertain where her life was headed and why it had taken such a devastating turn.

Today, ten years later, she says she's grateful to her ex-husband for helping her gain clarity and perspective. It turns out that she never liked or connected with Ohio, but because that was where her husband's family and business were based, she agreed to settle there. And that's just what she'd done—settled! She spent more than twenty years of her life living somewhere that didn't inspire her, and it wasn't until she was "forced out" that she felt free. I can happily report that today my friend is thriving in Denver. She's eating healthier and exercising often. She has a great job, and she regularly dates. She recently confessed that while she once felt she needed a man to be happy, she's discovered happiness on her own. She says,

"If he shows up—great. If not, I'll be just fine." Whenever her past marriage comes up in conversation, she refers to how things unfolded as a gift and nods her head emphatically when I say, "It was all part of the plan."

DÉJÀ VU

Are you familiar with déjà vu—that flashback feeling like you've *been here before*? As I understand it, déjà vu is Spirit impressing us with thoughts and feelings meant to remind us of our divine plan. When it occurs, it's meant to validate that we're on track and that our life is unfolding just as we scripted it. We're exactly where we should be!

CALLING FOR BACKUP

The truth is that there is a bigger picture, a master plan. Have faith that there's greater work at play, and when in doubt call on the unseen world to help reassure you that your life is unfolding intentionally. Ask your visiting spirit guides to help you spark divine faith, trust, and assurance within you.

My grandma Babe, whom I write about extensively in *Spirited,* appeared to me as a visiting spirit guide "on assignment" to help me when I was struggling in college to find my voice and discover my purpose. Grandma Babe's spirit was drawn to me at this time in my life because she'd similarly struggled in her own life. She'd battled with depression and, sadly and very tragically, eventually

VISITING GUIDES

Visiting or "temporary" spirit guides are enlightened spirits between lifetimes who feel bonded to us either based on our similar life experiences and particular interests or simply because they have a special affection for us. They work with us—coming and going—as we master specific life lessons. Throughout this period of learning and growing, they show up in our dreams, often disguised as teachers or mentors we once had. Their presence may be felt and sometimes seen in meditation. Other times, they "speak" through the people around us, using our trusted friends and family members as divine messengers to deliver important insights and truths. Our visiting guides stay present with us as long as needed, before moving on to assist someone else. This could be six days or six years. It doesn't matter to them—our guides have all the time in the world!

took her own life. She appeared to me as a guide to both help me learn from her mistakes and to help her balance out her karmic debt. Babe was committed to helping me, and she stuck around until I got on track toward fulfilling my purpose of serving others in my special woo-woo kind of way.

We each draw the guides to us who are most like us and who had similar life experiences and struggles. Our guides are here to serve us, and their insights are invaluable. Call on them to send you inspirational messages, prophetic dreams, and clear guidance. Think or say aloud:

Spirit Guides, thank you for being with me now, inspiring me with your divine guidance and wisdom. Help me move forward in complete faith and trust as I create a meaningful life that serves to fulfill my purpose for being.

I once did a reading for a client named Julie whose brother came through in spirit to communicate that he was working on the other side as a visiting guide to help their living mother. I saw him hovering above his mother with his hands held out, my sign for a spirit working on assignment to help the living. I was then clairvoyantly shown a flash of a Lifetime movie I'd just watched about an abusive relationship (yes, I love a tearjerker Lifetime movie). Upon hearing this, Julie confirmed that their mother was in a physically abusive relationship with an alcoholic man. In spirit, Julie's brother wanted Julie to know that she should not feel guilty about moving away. He clairvoyantly impressed upon me the image of a real estate sign and a passport, followed by a green light, my sign for GO! Julie confirmed that she'd moved overseas to Australia. Her brother wanted her to know that helping Mom was now *his* job. He was guiding her in her dreams, impressing her mind with truth and healing. Julie cried throughout the entire reading, and when it was over I could see a visible shift in her energy, as if a huge weight had been lifted off of her shoulders. She said she felt relieved and free of guilt, and she now understood that her mother's happiness and healing were not her responsibility. She also expressed gratitude that her mother was being supported by her brother, who would continue to help guide her forward from the spiritual realm.

PLACING THE CALL

In addition to calling on your visiting spirit guides, feel free to call on Archangel Uriel, known as the "Light of God," to heighten your trust as you tackle and try to resolve each of life's challenges. A patron angel of literature and music, Archangel Uriel gives us the gift of creative fire along with the power to expand our vision and see how the often puzzling pieces of our life fit perfectly together. Archangel Uriel is often depicted standing with a fiery sword at the gate of the "Lost Eden." His symbol is an open hand holding a flame, representing illumination. It's been said that Uriel helps us turn our worst disappointments into victories and blessings. He helps us to let go of the past, move forward, and forgive.

For years, I've called on Uriel in prayer and meditation, to light the way along my spiritual path and to help me make big and small transitions and changes in my daily life. He feels like a confident, reassuring caretaker who gracefully moves in, usually in front of me to lead the way. He's always holding some kind of light, either a lantern, a burning torch, or a flashlight. He appears as a fiery orange swirl of energy and light.

On days when you're struggling with skepticism, fear, or doubt, call on Archangel Uriel. Say aloud, or just think: *Archangel Uriel, thank you for filling me with the divine trust of God, thereby relieving me of all self-doubt and fear. May your presence light the way in helping me to resolve any challenges I might face, restoring order and faith in my life.*

rest assured: A RECAP

- We can't always see the beauty and the gifts within our everyday struggles and challenges, yet there truly is beauty and purpose—a divine plan in play.

- If we welcome life's struggles and challenges as opportunities to learn and grow, and rest assured that everything is happening just as it was intended, our perception experiences a seismic shift, and suddenly we're able to see the beauty and gifts in every situation—the desirable and the undesirable.

- Every event has a rhyme and a reason, including "untimely" and "tragic" deaths. Each has the potential to create a profound transformation for the living, provided that those left behind choose to learn from the experience and allow it to shift their own energy up toward love and light.

- In the ancient Kabbalah tradition, the expression of divine trust and assertion is referred to as *netzach,* and its energy resides in the sacral center, specifically the right hip. When *netzach* energy is unblocked and awakened, you can expect to feel a sense of determination, assertion, and personal conviction flowing freely within you.

· Have faith that there's greater work at play, and when in doubt call on your visiting spirit guides and the angelic realm to help reassure you that your life is unfolding intentionally. Call on Archangel Uriel to help awaken divine faith, trust, and assurance within you as you tackle and try to resolve each of your life's challenges.

STEP 8

RELINQUISH CONTROL

As you continue to trust that your life is flowing according to plan and continue to meet your challenges head-on with the intention of learning and growing from them, there may still be times when your doubts and fears object. You might find yourself questioning the bigger picture, the rhyme or reason behind certain situations and events, especially if they present a struggle for you. You might even grow impatient for the good life I keep promising you is up ahead. Well, would it help you to know that time and time again, the unseen world assures me that we've each been given the opportunity to receive an abundance of contentment, happiness, and purposeful fulfillment in our lives when we rest assured that there is a divine plan at work and then *relinquish control*? A common sentiment Spirit asks me to pass along to the living every day is: Let go and let life flow. Catchy, right? And it sounds simple enough; except that it isn't always. Surrendering resistance and relinquishing control over our day-to-day lives can be tough. And yet I've seen what happens when clients decide to stop resisting where they're at on the road of life and trust that they've been led and are being led exactly where they need to go. What they soon discover, and what I hope you'll similarly realize, is that almost as soon as we accept ourselves, the people, situations, and circumstances that have shown up in our lives, and put our faith in the divine plan, we start to feel *a whole lot better.*

I try really hard to practice what I preach, but I'll be honest—sometimes even I become impatient. When things don't go exactly my way—when our sitter cancels on us last-minute, forcing us to change our plans, or when I'm headed to the gym for a much needed workout and I get called into work early—I'll often catch myself reacting defensively, acting out with frustration, fear, and doubt. In other words, I become resistant to life. At times like these, my spirit guides remind me that this will get me nowhere. In meditation, they've compared resisting life to swimming upstream against a current. They've clairvoyantly showed me an image of myself standing waist-deep in a rushing river. The force of the current pushes against me, almost knocking me down, and it becomes instantly clear that trying to swim against the power of this natural current will be futile. My guides encourage me to turn downstream and let go. I do, and what a relief it is! The current carries me gently and easily along. This is what it feels like to relinquish control and be in the flow of life.

Almost instantly, when you relinquish control, your life will begin to effortlessly and easily move forward.

Don't be surprised when the right situations and people begin to magically appear. When you're in the flow, synchronicities become a regular, day-to-day occurrence. Instead of feeling that life is a constant upstream struggle, when you relinquish control and let go, you begin to experience an almost effortless unfolding and divine timing to everything in your life.

A client named Courtney who lost her forty-something husband to cancer was struggling with grief, the unfair and "untimely" departure of his death. Courtney confided in me that she felt absolutely lost without her husband and was afraid she couldn't manage on her own. It didn't help that she was battling with her teenage sons, who were acting out; she was isolating herself from her family and friends, insisting she didn't need their help and support; and she was using food to stuff down her grief, fear, and resentment. In spirit her husband came through immediately, along with Courtney's deceased mother, who had also lost her husband to cancer at a young age (this is no coincidence, by the way!). Both of them had a strong message for Courtney: *Let go! Stop clinging to the past and what woulda, coulda, or shoulda happened.* Courtney's husband wanted me to assure Courtney that his death was "right on time." He clairvoyantly showed me the number 47. Courtney validated that this was the age at which he died. Courtney's husband wanted her to recognize that his death was an opportunity for her to learn a valuable life lesson: Stop resisting and fighting life. Relinquish control—*let go*—and embrace the opportunity to grow stronger on your own. He clairvoyantly showed me a lion, my sign for strength.

He then flashed in my mind's eye a bunch of puzzle pieces laid out in front of Courtney. I told her, "You have everything you need to put your life back together. You do not need your husband to make you whole." Hearing this message, Courtney looked like she'd been startled awake. Once she had a minute to digest what I'd told her and accept the information, she let out a long and exhausted sigh of relief. She sobbed uncontrollably for a few minutes and then confided in me that for the first time since her husband's death she felt like everything would be okay.

SET IT

Set the intention now to relinquish control over your life by awakening the divine expression of surrender and acceptance within you. Trust that you've been led to where you are now for a reason, even if you're not sure exactly what that is, and let go of any inclination you may have to control what comes next.

Relinquishing control and trusting in divine timing can make even the most patient of us a little bit antsy. The Universal Law of Gestation states that everything takes time to manifest, and the time varies depending on how much, and *what kind* of, energy you give to the manifestation. This means that if you're feeling particularly anxious about how quickly a situation is or is not unfolding, consider that what makes a stew so tasty isn't quick cooking, but the fact that the ingredients have a chance to *stew*, and sometimes this takes a while. If this doesn't give you the comfort you crave, but only whets your appetite, then consider energetically speeding up the unfolding process by following a practice I call "Set It and Forget It." Truly, this is a great cosmic shortcut!

SET IT AND FORGET IT

Before we begin, I should make the point: Relinquishing control does not mean you do nothing and sit back as a passive player, an outside observer of your own life. On the contrary, your role in life is meant to be active and engaged, one in which you do your best to set yourself in exactly the direction you want to go, and then, you let go.

You can greatly influence what comes into your life, and when, by first asserting what it is that you want for yourself. Whatever that is—to have a child, travel to another country, meet your soul mate, get hired for your dream job, achieve financial security, enjoy good health— it's important you become crystal clear about what it is that you want. Once you have a grasp on what that is, you then focus your attention on *why* you want it. Understanding why you want something reveals the *feeling* you most desire. For example, if you desire to have children, what's fueling your desire? Will children bring more joy to your life? Renew your sense of wonder? Give your life more meaning? Identify what you want and *why*. That's all you need to know. While we cannot anticipate or control exactly where our lives are headed, we can ask for what we desire. So assert that for yourself, either by writing it down, talking it out, or praying or meditating on it, and then actively release everything else—the when, where, who, and how. These are just details and totally out of your control.

SET IT

It's very easy to get hung up on the details, especially how a situation will unfold, and if you're not careful, this hang-up will create resistance (just like that upstream current I described) that will slow down the unfolding process. In other words, when you try to control how something happens by either forcing a situation or preventing it from unfolding naturally, you actually get in the way of allowing it to happen at all. Holding on to control actually *holds back* the unfolding process. This goes for the big and small stuff alike. Certainly you're familiar with the saying "Don't sweat the small stuff." This isn't just a popular catchphrase. These are truly words to live by, because what happens when we sweat little things is that we create tension in our body—energetic resistance that blocks the flow of life.

SPIRITS DON'T SWEAT THE SMALL STUFF

Who better to confirm the validity of this message than the man who coined it? I stood before an audience of five hundred in Beverly Hills, California. I'd just opened the door to the spirit world, and the first bright light to appear at the front of the line was a spirit named Richard.

I clairaudiently heard his name and claircognizantly understood that this was a highly evolved spirit. I said, "Does anyone know a man who was very enlightened in life and served as a spiritual teacher of some sort? He died from a heart issue, I believe. He's also showing me books." A woman in the audience stood up, and as she did, the light of this spirit hovered over her head. She confirmed that her husband Richard had died of a pulmonary embolism while flying during a book tour. She said that her husband was Richard Carlson, "the man who wrote the book *Don't Sweat the Small Stuff*." I gasped out loud, because I'd just bought this book for my own husband two months prior. I was thrilled to be communicating with this enlightened spirit who strongly impressed upon me that his death was actually right on time, despite his relatively young age. He'd completed what he came to Earth to do—he'd passed on an important life lesson to millions who needed it (*Don't Sweat the Small Stuff* became one of the fastest-selling books in publishing history and was a *New York Times* bestseller for nearly two years). Richard impressed upon me that within his relatively short life, he'd completed his "life's work," and now he was watching over his two daughters and wife from the other side, lovingly guiding them along.

I'm sure you've experienced a day like this: You wake up late—*ugh*—and in your frustrated mad scramble to get out the door, you can't find your cell phone, your car keys, or both! After turning the house upside down, you finally find them (they were in your bag), but by now you're really running late. You jump in the car, jam on the gas, and then proceed to hit every red light on your way to work. Once you finally arrive, you can't believe your bad luck—no parking spaces! Sound familiar? We've all had mornings like this, and it has nothing to do with bad luck. A chain of events like this doesn't happen by chance. A morning like this happens when we sweat the big and small stuff, when we create energetic resistance that jams the natural unfolding and flow of our lives.

A client of mine had just listed her home for sale, and she expressed her fear that because she lived in a buyers' real estate market, she wouldn't receive full asking price. In fact, she was pretty convinced that the eventual outcome wouldn't be financially beneficial at all. I agreed that she might be right. She may not get her full asking price. "On the other hand," I told her, "if you change your attitude about it, you just might get exactly what you want."

While there's really no way to know what any outcome will be, we each have the power to deliberately set things in motion in the direction we want them to go, by first releasing our fears about how things *could* go wrong and focusing on what's already going right. I said to my client, "Perhaps you have a competent and confident real estate agent who assures you that your house will sell? And didn't you tell me that you added a master bath and updated your kitchen—upgrades that'll no doubt add value to your home? Focus on what's going right, and then, relinquish control."

Once you release and empty yourself of fear-based thoughts and feelings, like *I can't . . . I won't . . . I don't de-*

serve it, you make space for *I can . . . I will . . . I'm worthy. I deserve everything I want and need!* When you scrap your fear and resistance (this goes back to Step 5: Release) and get into a positive state of allowing and receiving, you dramatically increase the likelihood of getting exactly what you want and need. Add to that the fact that as you wait in eager anticipation and excitement, believing that whatever you desire is on the way, and express gratitude and appreciation *ahead of time* for getting what you've asked for, you energetically speed up the unfolding process.

FORGET IT

Do everything in your power to set yourself in exactly the direction you want to go; and then forget about it, that is—*let go*—and be open to receive whatever shows up. The reality is that the eventual outcome of any situation may look surprisingly different from what you asked for. What Spirit has communicated to me is that the people, events, and circumstances that show up in our lives are based on what will best help us spiritually grow and evolve, and the truth is—we don't always know what's in our best interest! I have this recurring dream where I'm behind the wheel of a car and every attempt to control where I'm going ends badly. Long lights, bumper-to-bumper traffic, dead ends. Almost as soon as I'm about to lose it, my spirit guides arrive on the scene and kindly suggest I hop in the backseat. Once they take control of the wheel, I relax, knowing they'll safely deliver me wherever I need to go.

I once read a woman named Liz whose deceased father-in-law came through right away with a message about his grandson. I was clairsentiently impressed with a strong feeling of a bossy, overbearing, out-of-control kid, along with a clip from the movie *Parenthood* with Steve Martin, which is my sign for the chaos and challenges that accompany real parenthood. "Is your son acting out?" I asked Liz.

Liz confirmed that she and her husband Jason had recently started couples therapy to help them develop better parenting skills for coping with their son, Collin. I told her, "Dad is saying it's not about Collin. Rather, he's acting out to help your husband with unresolved issues."

Through claircognizance, I had an overwhelming knowing that his father had emotionally abandoned Liz's husband, Jason, when he was a young boy. I was shown the number 7. I had a strong feeling that Jason and Collin were karmically connected. "How old is Collin now?" I asked. Liz told me he was seven. After several more insights provided by Spirit, it became clear to me that part of Collin's contract was to help his dad break the pattern of dysfunction between father and son by providing Jason with an opportunity to express and extend to Collin the loving-kindness Jason hadn't received. Except, Jason hadn't done that. Instead, he was unconsciously following in his father's footsteps. His demanding work schedule kept him on the road and physically distant from his son. When he was home, he was distracted and emotionally disconnected. As a result, Collin was acting out. He was using bad behavior to get his dad's attention and *wake him up!* This story is a perfect example of how situations and events often unfold very differently from how we imagine they will. Originally, Liz and Jason sought out therapy to help them with their son, but it turned out that it was Jason who most needed the healing work.

Relinquishing control takes an admission on your part that you simply cannot control every detail of your life or predict exactly where you're headed. And isn't that a relief? You can only know and do so much, so relax! Give yourself a break. Whether you're trying to sell a house, fix a relationship, land a job, or lose ten pounds, what Spirit assures me is that there's a limit to what you can individually do to shape the course of your life. We can take actionable steps to position ourselves in the direction we want to go (set it), and then we must simply let go (forget it). When you relinquish control over exactly how your future will unfold, concentrate your focus only on the best possible outcome, and go about your life with an upbeat, optimistic "What will be will be" attitude, you really can't lose!

AWAKEN SURRENDER AND ACCEPTANCE

The following EnLighten Up meditation is designed to further awaken and lighten the energy in your sacral center, the space between your hips, so that surrender and acceptance can easily flow through you. Think of this energy center as an upside-down triangle with three points to light up. The point at your right hip awakens faith and trust, the point at your left awakens surrender and acceptance, and the point at the base of your pelvis awakens your divine power (Step 9).

Our sacral centers need extra lightening and brightening because that's where so many of us feel blocked. Do you feel tight in the hips? Most of us do, and this is because having faith and trust, relinquishing control, and reclaiming our personal power is no easy feat. It's hard and uncomfortable work, and for this reason many of us resist it. Over time this resistance creates an energetic bottleneck, a tightness that has no doubt contributed to the current yoga craze.

The meditations for Steps 8, 9, and 10 are designed to loosen, open, and ultimately release any energy that's gotten stuck within your hips. In the Kabbalah tradition, the energy associated with your left hip is called *hod,* and when it's awakened and unblocked, you can expect to feel

ENLIGHTEN UP:

Open Your Hips

Close your eyes and take several deep breaths in through your nose and out through your mouth. With each breath, focus on relaxing your entire body, from the top of your head down through your feet. Imagine yourself out in nature as a magnificent tree, feet firmly rooted in the earth and your head reaching high into the sky. Take several more deep, relaxing breaths to firmly center and ground you in this natural space. Once you feel centered and grounded, focus your attention on your sacral center, specifically the pocket of energy in your left hip, located within the extensive root system of the Tree of Life.

Continue to breathe.

Now visualize that a spark of amber-orange light begins to glow in your left hip pocket. With each inhalation, imagine this amber-orange light filling up the area there. Allow this space to soften and open. Feel the light expand, loosen, open, and unblock any stuck energy, so that the divine light of surrender and acceptance can flow freely through your energetic body.

Breathe deeply and easily.

Set the intention to surrender control and resistance and accept the things you cannot change.

Throughout the rest of your day, let your breath serve as a reminder that you're an extension of God, and as such, the expression of divine acceptance resides within you. If you forget or doubt this, repeat mentally or out loud: *Everything happens in divine timing and according to divine will when I let go.*

an energetic shift within your emotional body, felt primarily as a sense of relief and a renewed sense of security.

When left hip energy is blocked, in addition to possessing a tendency to control people and events, you may also suffer from emotional and sexual guilt. Remember the story about my client Courtney, who'd come to me mourning the untimely loss of her husband? Well, when I delivered the news that his death was actually right on time and that her husband in spirit wanted her to let go and move on with her life, I sensed a lightening of her energy right away and saw a physical shift in her body. She uncrossed her arms and legs and sat easier and more comfortably in her chair. I didn't think much of it at the time, just filed the information away, but then when a year later she returned for a follow-up reading, she happily reported that once she'd let go of the guilt and grief tied to her husband's passing, she felt free to move on to the next chapter in her life—finding a new romantic partner. Not long after our reading, she said, she began to feel more receptive and emotionally open to other people. I smiled at this. What I wanted to tell her but resisted (boundaries, people!) was that the energy in her sacral center was flowing again, and with it a renewed desire for intimacy had awakened within.

In another instance, I worked with a man named Jeff who was in the closet about his sexual orientation, and while he did a fairly good job of hiding his true colors in the real world, as soon as he asked for guidance from the unseen world, his truth came to light. Right off the bat, his deceased grandfather came through and clairvoyantly showed me a rainbow, my sign for being gay. Grandpa also impressed me with an image of Jeff standing tall and wearing a smile on his face, and I clairsentiently felt a wave of unconditional love and acceptance wash over me. Grandpa's message was clear: *Let go of the world's expectations of you. Stop trying to control who you are by acting like someone else. Be proud.* Hearing this, Jeff broke down in tears. He admitted that he'd repressed and tried to control who he was his entire life. Now his grandfather was giving him permission to be himself, with no explanations, apologies, or shame attached. Jeff said he finally felt free, and he walked out of my office that day a changed man. A couple of years later, he revisited me for a follow-up reading. He told me that since he'd come out, all areas of his life had changed for the better. On the relationship front, he'd found the perfect partner.

DON'T FORGET THE LESSON

So what happens when you relinquish control of the details, put your faith and trust in divine timing and the bigger plan, and then the events that unfold are not to your liking? I've had clients express frustration that after they've "let go" their life doesn't feel like it's coming together in a complete and perfect way. "What's the deal?" they want to know. "Why does my life still feel challenging and difficult? Did I miss something?"

What I tell them is: The thing you might be missing is *the lesson*.

Truly, every challenge in your life has intention. It's shown up for a reason—not just to serve as aggravation and screw with your day. So if, after you relinquish control, life continues to unfold in a way that feels challenging and difficult, chances are very good that you're being faced with an important life lesson, and until you confront it head-on and learn from it, it will continue to show up and block your way. So take a moment now and clarify what about your life continues to feel hard. Relationships? Financial security? Career fulfillment? Your physical health?

I was in Scottsdale on a girls' trip with some high school pals to celebrate our thirty-fifth birthdays. My friend Shana and I were sitting at the pool talking about her golden ratio tattoo. I asked what it meant and she gave me a long astrological explanation. I said, "So to sum up: It represents 'balance.'" As I was saying the word, she said it simultaneously. We laughed, and I told her I've always known that one of my key life lessons is to learn balance. I'm always juggling, and depending on the day, I may have five balls up in the air that I'm trying desperately not to drop. Later that night, as we were headed out to dinner, I opened the door of our hotel room just as a huge tarantula was walking past the doorway. Only in Arizona! After getting over a sudden case of the creepy-crawlies, I realized the spider must be a message from Spirit (I can't help it; my mind just *goes there*). On the cab ride to the restaurant, on my iPhone I looked up animal totems and the symbolic significance of tarantulas and was provided with the following explanation: "A spider totem teaches you balance: between past and future, physical and spirit, male and female." So there ya go—Spirit had sent me a spider to validate what I believed to be true: One of my life lessons is to learn balance.

Whatever's challenging you, rest assured that life is serving up exactly what you need, when you need it. Can you accept this? If your answer is no, consider this: If you want your life to change, to flow, to unfold differently than it has up to this point, then you must surrender. *Stop resisting your life.* Philosopher Lao-Tzu, the father of Taoism, said, "Life is a series of natural and spontaneous changes. Don't resist them—that only creates sorrow. Let reality be reality. Let things flow naturally forward in whatever way they like." Accept that you are where you are with good reason. There's a lesson to be learned, an opportunity to grow. The people, situations, and circumstances of your life have shown up at exactly this time to teach you something valuable. Do you know what that is?

◄o►

James was suffering from chronic back pain when a co-worker offered to give him some prescription pain medication. James accepted. He took a couple and put the rest of the pills in an old empty aspirin bottle that he brought home. Not aware of their potential danger, he shelved the pills in his medicine cabinet and soon forgot about them. When his fourteen-year-old son Ryan came down with a common cold a few months later, he took a handful of them, thinking they were aspirin. He accidentally overdosed.

For years after the accident, James blamed himself for his son's death. His paralyzing grief and guilt led him to counseling. He also sought the advice of his parish priest. Eventually, he attended one of my small group readings that consisted of ten people.

Days before the reading, I'd felt the relentless presence of a spirit insisting that he speak with his father. The night of the reading, there he was again, so I led off by asking if anyone knew a young boy named Ryan. I'd clairaudiently heard his name. James raised his hand. I said, "His presence is strong and he wants you to know that he is fine, very happy and safe. He also wants you to know he doesn't blame you. He's saying, 'Let it go, Dad. I was going to go anyway.' To let you know his spirit is with you, he's messed with one of your clocks. [Remember, Spirit often interferes in seemingly trivial ways to prove to the living that they are for real.] He says it stopped on a significant time and you'll know what this means. Does that make any sense?" James didn't get the reference at the time, but then I later received this note:

> Before I left the reading [you] told me that Ryan had messed with a clock in our home. I went home that night to check out all of our clocks. . . . The hands on the clock on our dining room table had stopped on the number 8:23—the date of Ryan's death. I am a very analytical person with my own legal practice, and in my mind the clock was irrefutable evidence that the messages of love and acceptance from our son were real. That moment I knew that he truly did not blame me, that he was safe and that we would be together again.

When I did a follow-up reading for James, this time by phone, I could feel a considerable lightness in his energy and warmth in his voice. He told me that his faith in God and what lies beyond had been restored. He'd moved out of his deep depression and regained his will to live, and he'd actively gotten involved in supporting other families who had similarly suffered a loss, by sharing what he'd learned about death and what happens next.

CALLING FOR BACKUP

If you haven't yet realized what the challenges in your life are trying to teach you or had that aha moment when finally you say, "Now I get it!" then simply pray for clarity. Ask your visiting spirit guides to reveal, and help you learn, the lesson at hand.

Mentally give them permission to intervene in your life and ask that they help you relinquish control and give you faith and trust that your life is unfolding just as it's meant to. Think or say aloud: *Spirit Guides, I acknowledge your presence and ask that you assist me in letting go. Thank you for inspiring surrender and acceptance within and around me, while helping me to embrace change and go with the flow of life.*

PLACING THE CALL

In addition to asking your visiting guides to help you surrender your fears and doubts and accept where you are, call on Archangel Raziel, known as the "prince of knowledge of hidden things." He's also fittingly called the "angel of mysteries" and has a reputation for helping people trust in divine timing. Say aloud, or just think: *Archangel Raziel, please help me to open my mind and heart to greater spiritual awareness and understanding. Please help me to release and let go of any limiting beliefs, doubts, worries, and fears that may be keeping me blocked or stuck. Thank you for filling me with faith and trust that everything in my life is unfolding according to Divine plan, and for guiding me along and validating for me that I'm on the right path.*

In 2004, when Brian and I lived in Santa Monica, I stumbled upon Angel Raziel one day. We were walking along Ocean Avenue when I spotted a book on the ground. The title of the book was *Sepher Raziel Hamalach: The Book of the Angel Raziel,* and while I'm not versed in Hebrew nor had I ever heard of Angel Raziel, I picked the book up anyway and took it home. Eight years later—would you believe I still have this book? There have been times when I've boxed that book up to move into a new office or house and I've thought, *Why am I keeping this around? I can't even read it!*

Well, now I understand why.

Back in 2001 when I first found the book, I was in the early stages of developing my gift. I had a lot of questions: *Is my gift really real? Can I make a living talking to the dead? Is this crazy work or my true calling and purpose?* Archangel Raziel heard my fear and doubt and "sent me" his book as a sign to make his presence known and also inspire me to believe in myself and the divine plan. And while I didn't understand his significance then, when I look back now I see clearly how his presence synchronistically coincided with a big shift in my skepticism. Not long after Archangel Raziel "appeared," I began to really trust that something much bigger than me was driving my life forward with purpose.

relinquish: A RECAP

- Holding on to control actually holds back the unfolding process. When you relinquish control, your life will begin to effortlessly and easily move forward. Don't be surprised when the right situations and people begin to magically appear, and when synchronicities become a regular, day-to-day occurrence.

- Relinquishing control does not mean you do nothing and sit back as a passive player, an outside observer of your own life. On the contrary, your role in life is meant to be active and engaged, where you do your best to set yourself in exactly the direction you want to go (set it), and then, you let go (forget it).

- The reality is that the eventual outcome of any situation may look surprisingly different from what you asked for. The people, events, and circumstances that show up in our lives are based on what will best help us spiritually grow and evolve.

- In the ancient Kabbalah tradition, the expression of divine surrender is referred to as *hod,* and its energy resides in the sacral center, specifically the left hip. When *hod* energy is awakened and unblocked, you can expect to feel an energetic shift within your emotional body, felt primarily as a sense of relief and a renewed sense of security flowing freely within you.

· In addition to asking your spirit guides to help you surrender your fears and doubts, call on the angelic realm. For a conduit of *hod* energy, call on Archangel Raziel, known as the "prince of knowledge of hidden things." Ask that he help you relinquish control and give you faith and trust that your life is unfolding just as it's meant to.

STEP 9

RECLAIM YOUR POWER

Once you surrender to the reality that you cannot control or predict every detail and eventual outcome of your life, and when you accept what you truly are—a spiritual being temporarily residing in a physical body to travel life's roadways, with the sole purpose to learn, grow, and surpass your own expectations—then you can focus on doing *just that*.

But the question remains: How?

By just being you.

While we all share God's powerful DNA, we're also individual expressions of God. Meaning, there's no one else quite like you. So set the intention now to become clear on exactly what strengths and talents make you unique. When you know who and what you are, you reclaim your power and you feel *empowered* to move forward with clarity, confidence, and conviction, along with a joyful sense of divine purpose.

What most people don't realize is that true power comes from being grounded and standing firmly in your truth, which is just another way of saying that true power comes from knowing exactly who you are and what you're capable of. Ramana Maharshi, a great teacher in the yogic tradition, said that to attain inner freedom one must continuously and sincerely ask the question: "Who am I?"

WHO ARE YOU?

Each of us is born with the same purpose—to express and extend God's love and light. This is our life's "work," and while we all have a similar job to do, specifically what we do and how we do it varies from person to person based on our individual strengths and talents. Recognizing your uniqueness is what many in my woo-woo psychic circles call "standing firmly in your truth" and "aligning with your purpose." All this means is that the key to living a purposeful life lies in identifying how best you can be a vehicle for God's divine love and light. The wise Viktor Frankl said, "Everyone has his own specific vocation or mission in life; everyone must carry out a concrete assignment that demands fulfillment. Therein he cannot be replaced, nor can his life be repeated, thus, everyone's task is unique as his specific opportunity to implement it." In other words—you've got an important job to do that only *you can do*. Do you know what that is?

Not sure? Welcome to the human race.

What I see day after day in the faces of the people I pass on the street, stand in line behind at my neighborhood

Starbucks, and sweat alongside at the gym is a like-minded look of disconnect. So many of us still haven't connected the dots between who we are and what we're meant to do in this life. So many of us simply don't know what it means to be human, and as a result we feel utterly lost. We drive around in circles, go left when we should go right, chase after relationships, careers, and physical and monetary goals that only lead to unfulfilling dead ends.

We all know someone whose life choices have seemed misguided, don't we? The guy, for example, who chases the dream of becoming an actor when everyone around him can clearly see that his temperament and skills are more suited for teaching third grade math. I once knew someone like this—she used to stare back at me in the mirror every morning! Thankfully, Grandma Babe came through when she did and helped me recognize my unique radiance, my true calling. And yet I'm no different, no more special than you. If our life's work is to express and extend our radiance—God's love and light—then I've just figured out the best way for me to get the job done. Understand that we each approach life's work differently. For some it may be through art; others might be called to heal, while others gravitate toward teaching, science, or business.

In what direction do you feel called? Ask yourself, *What is it that I love to do? What am I naturally good at? What comes easy?* It's important that you let go of other people's projections of who you should be and what you should do. Instead, go inward. Don't think, *feel*. What does your intuitive wisdom tell you? Ask yourself, *What lights me up and makes me feel alive?*

When you do whatever it is you were born to do in this

lifetime, you'll know it. When you're "standing firmly in your truth" and "aligned with your purpose," your life expands from one of mere existence where you're going through the day-to-day motions, to one where you're excited and lit up each and every day.

Amy, a girlfriend of mine, shared that her parents had dedicated their professional lives to the medical field. Her mother was a nurse and her dad was a well-known doctor. Both of her parents expected Amy to follow in their footsteps, and since Amy believed she was wired like they were, she willingly took steps toward fulfilling their expectations. She earned a prestigious degree, and soon after, she accepted an internship position in a renowned hospital, working on a groundbreaking trial. She was on her way! Except she was bored out of her mind. Every day, as she walked the halls of the hospital, she dreamed about doing something else, something that felt *more like her*. After months and months of struggling with her chosen career path, Amy left medicine to pursue floral design. Needless to say, her dad was bewildered and not at all pleased. But Amy didn't care because she soon discovered that working as a florist lit her up in a way that medicine never had. It awakened her spirit. When friends and colleagues questioned this rather unexpected career change, she simply explained that floral design felt right.

Amy's been managing her own business for eight years now. She's as happy as can be. She says her dad still shakes his head, not understanding why she wouldn't want to do something "bigger," and she just smiles. She doesn't expect him to get it. Medicine is all he knows, and it's what he was called to do. Amy was called in a different direction, and neither road is better than the other. Amy's truth was not her father's, and his was not hers. Big deal. You see, it's not what you do that's important; what matters most is expressing your divine and unique radiance *whatever you do.*

I once made a connection with the spirit of a man who ended his life after suffering for years from severe depression. Through clairvoyance and clairsentience, he communicated to me that it wasn't until he died and went through a life review process that he fully understood the root of his unhappiness—he hadn't lived his truth. He'd worn the mask of a successful lawyer. Like Amy, he had followed in the footsteps of his father, pursuing a professional path that from a young age he'd felt was expected of him. And yet what he really wanted to do was be a musician. Music called to him, but sadly he never followed the calling and spent many years being frustrated, resentful, lonely, and ultimately, unfulfilled.

In what direction do you feel called? What do you ache for? What sustains you? If you, too, are guilty of wearing a mask that only serves to cover your divine radiance within, or if you're still struggling with self-doubt, unclear about what your unique gifts are and where your talents are meant to take you, try answering the following questions to help spark clarity within:

1. What makes you smile? (activities, people, events, hobbies, projects, etc.)
2. What were your favorite things to do in the past? What about now?
3. What activities make you lose track of time?

4. What makes you feel great about yourself?
5. Who inspires you most? (family, friends, authors, artists, leaders, etc.) Which qualities inspire you in each person?
6. What are you naturally good at? (skills, abilities, gifts, etc.)
7. What do people typically ask you for help in?
8. If you had to teach something, what would you teach?
9. If you could effectively get a message across to a large group of people, who would those people be?
10. What would you regret not fully doing, being, or having in your life?

If you're still unclear how best to express your unique radiance, ask yourself, *Who aren't I? What road don't I want to go down?* According to the Universal Law of Polarity, everything has an opposite. In readings, I simply cannot tell you how often spirits support the law of polarity when offering relationship advice. For example, I once read a woman named Ellen who confided in me up front that she was seeking help from the unseen world about her current relationship. I was clairvoyantly shown a vision of a messy room, which is my sign for sloppy. I said, "Are you dating a guy who's sloppy, unclean, or who you consider to be emotionally a mess?" She tentatively nodded her head. I got the strong claircognizant impression from Spirit that her current relationship was meant to provide her with clarity and direction. I said, "It looks like your current boyfriend has shown up in your life to serve as an exam-

IDENTIFYING RADIANCE:

Holly's Story

In a reading with Rebecca a few years ago, she mentioned that my husband would start a business and that everyone would be telling us it was too risky and not to pursue it, but she said it would be very successful. At that time, my husband was working for a company with no plans to start one of his own. About a year later, he came up with a business plan that he was really passionate about. We struggled for the first three years, and just like Rebecca said, everyone told us to give up. The only thing that kept me going was remembering Rebecca's words! After three years, we are finally successful and enjoying every minute of it. What a blessing to do work that you love!

ple of the *opposite* of what you need." Her guides clairvoyantly showed me ducks in a row, my sign for organization. I told Ellen, "They're telling me that you're meant to be with someone who matches your level of cleanliness and order."

Polarity helps us clarify. When you know what you don't want, you become clearer on what you do want. Likewise, when you know who you aren't, you know who you are.

So who are you? Once you identify and embrace your unique radiance, and then use your special gifts and talents with the pure intention of serving others and spreading love, you're fulfilling your purpose—what you were born in this life to do.

I'm constantly reminded by my guides to "just be me."

No kidding, I clairaudiently hear them whisper these very words into my ear. They've been drilling this message into my head for as long as I can remember. Before any reading I do, whether for an individual or a group of three hundred, I quietly repeat these words, trust in them, and relax into *myself*. As soon as I do, I become a clear and open conduit for Spirit, able to pass along important messages from the dead to the living. The profound healing and transformation that my natural abilities provide are my validation that *just being me* is the purposeful work I'm meant to do in this lifetime.

STANDING IN YOUR TRUTH:

Beverly's Story

When I was around thirty-five I had a strong feeling that there was something that I was supposed to be doing, but I didn't know what it was. As I pondered this, an answer came into my mind that said that I would find out when I was forty. I thought, *But that is so far away.* I soon put this guidance out of my mind and continued with my life.

Fast-forward several years and it's the week before I turned forty-one and my knee got blown out playing a friendly game of basketball at my son's birthday party. I didn't know it at the time but my ACL was completely torn. The pain was so intense that I could not catch my breath, but eventually I got up and walked it off. At the time I was working construction and I continued with my regular life again, but the injury did force me to slow down a bit. Then the idea came into my mind to become a massage therapist. That was the weirdest thing ever. It was completely out of nowhere. I had never considered anything even remotely like that and was not a "people person" or even very sociable for that matter. But the idea persisted. So I found a school and signed up for a class to try it out. Well, right away I was hooked. It felt so right.

I was always receiving solicitations in the mail for various massage and therapy seminars. One day one came for a John F. Barnes Myofascial Release seminar. I had never heard of the man or Myofascial Release. But I felt compelled to take the seminar. That feeling would not go away and was so compelling that I couldn't resist it. So I finally gave in and signed up for the seminar. Once again, it felt so right.

I became a Myofascial Release therapist, which is what I continue to do now five years later. I know that I am working with my "truth." I absolutely love my healing work and it never feels like work. It is as if I am just visiting with a friend every time that I see a client.

I have learned that it is best to listen to the information that I receive, then be, allow, and go with the flow. There is always guidance available if we are only willing to allow and accept it.

AWAKEN YOUR TRUTH AND POWER

The following EnLighten Up meditation is designed to help you reclaim your personal power by sparking the energy at the base of your sacral center. In the ancient Kabbalah tradition, this energy is called *yesod,* and when it's awakened and unblocked, you can expect to feel an energetic shift primarily as a rekindled childlike sense of wonder, creativity, and excitement, along with joy for simply being alive. Once the energy at the base of your pelvis is fully unblocked and flowing freely within you, expect to feel solid in the foundation of who you are. Expect to feel powerful!

ENLIGHTEN UP:

Release Your Hips

Close your eyes and breathe slowly in through your nose and exhale slowly out through your mouth. Imagine yourself in your favorite natural setting. Become aware of your six senses. What do you hear, smell, see, touch, and taste? What do you intuitively feel and know? Take several more deep, relaxing breaths to firmly center and ground you in this natural space.

Return to the visualization of yourself as a magnificent tree, feet planted on the ground and growing roots into the earth. With each breath, feel your energetic body expanding, becoming bigger, stronger, and taller. Imagine your head reaching high into the sky. Now visualize a slow-burning amber-orange flame in your sacral center.

With each inhalation, visualize this light becoming a burning fire in between your hips. Feel the light unblock and release any remaining stagnant energy in this area of your body, so that divine power can flow freely within you.

Breathe deeply and easily.

Set the intention to stand firmly in your truth, reclaim your power, and open yourself up to the beauty, sweetness, spontaneity, and joys of life.

Throughout the rest of your day, let your breath serve as a reminder that you're an extension of God, and as such, divine power resides within you. If you forget or doubt this, repeat mentally or out loud: *It is safe for me to stand firmly in my truth, empowered as a child of God, filled with the grace of God. I am extending this love and light in everything I think, do, and say, and I have the power to live my life with purpose and meaning.*

CALLING FOR BACKUP

You've looked into the reflective pool and recognized who you truly are. From this day forward, call on the angelic realm, your "permanent" spirit guides, and deceased loved ones, to assist you in consciously showing up every day to do the job you were born to do, acting as a unique expression and extension of God by *just being you*.

Your permanent spirit guides are different from your visiting guides in that they've been with you since the day you were born and will continue to guide you throughout your lifetime, until you're ready to make the trip back home. As it is with your guardian angel, your permanent guides are in it for the long haul. They will never leave you and they're 100 percent committed to you. And because your permanent guides were once flesh and blood and had a similar personality and temperament as you, they can greatly empathize with you. Not only that, but also whatever your unique and particular talents, you have at least one permanent guide who also shares your gift and who inspires you to share it. Pretty cool, right?

One of my permanent guides is named Star. She clairaudiently revealed her name to me long ago. She appears to me as a golden silhouette radiating love and light and emanating pure joy. She also has beautiful long and wavy dark curls. What can I say—she's like the best version of me on a good hair day! She most often shows up in my dreams and meditations right before I'm scheduled to perform a large audience reading or appear on television. She works wonders at calming my nerves and is quick to remind me why I do this wild and crazy work. She often shows me stars as a sign she's working with me. In the restaurant my husband and I ate at after my first *Spirited* book reading, I saw a large star projected onto the floor, acknowledging a job well done. This guide often shows me the letters S-T-A-R on personalized license plates and billboards at times when I'm feeling shy or insecure and need a power boost.

In readings, a client's permanent guides will make their presence easily known. They often appear close to the side of the person they're guiding, much like a mother protecting her child. They clairvoyantly appear to me in human form rather than as an angelic ball of light, and they also tend to make their voices loud and clear. Meaning, they aren't afraid to speak up and communicate important truths on behalf of the person they're watching over. For example, during a reading with a woman named Janeen, I claivoyantly saw two guides: a tall, father-figure presence holding a staff firmly in his right hand and an Indian woman with her arms crossed. Both of these guides appeared directly to the left and right of Janeen, almost like they were hooked into her, indicating to me that they were her permanent guides. They then clairvoyantly showed me a man standing over Janeen casting a dark shadow on her light. I clairsentiently felt that Janeen's guides did not approve of this man and how he was treating Janeen. When I described what I was seeing to Janeen, she confirmed that her husband of more than twenty years had recently become emotionally and mentally abusive. I asked her guides for more insight into his behavior and was clairvoyantly shown the silhouette of a woman (not Janeen) standing next to Janeen's husband, indicating that there was another woman in the picture. I asked Janeen if she thought her husband was involved with another woman, and she admitted she'd feared that might be the case. Janeen's guides then clairvoyantly showed me a piano. I asked her, "Do you play the piano?" Janeen said it had always been a passion of hers. I clairsentiently felt an overwhelming sense of joy and fulfillment rise up in me as her guides showed me this piano and a stack of sheet music. I said, "Your guides are impressing on me that you should pursue music. It lights you up. It empowers you." I explained to Janeen that music specifically raises her energy. "Regardless of your husband's actions

238 · Rebecca Rosen

or the eventual outcome of your marriage, remember to play the piano if you're feeling down. Your musical gifts will lift you up."

In another reading, for a woman named Deanna, her father in spirit came through and clairvoyantly showed me a camera. I asked her, "Did you just get a new camera?" and Deanna said that photography had always been a passion of hers. In fact, her husband had just given her a camera for a birthday gift. I was then impressed with a strong feeling of fulfillment and clairvoyantly saw her father waving her forward, indicating she pursue photography. I told her, "Dad is saying to stick with it. It's taking you somewhere." Years after our reading, Deanna sent me this e-mail. . . .

> *Your reading changed my life. We had financial difficulty and lost our home in 2008, but we are now on our way back to home ownership and it is because of my success in photography that I am now able to help my family out financially. . . . [My photography] has also given me an outlet to grieve the death of my father.*

Of our permanent guides, there's usually a leader of the pack, a "gatekeeper" who keeps all the spiritual energy surrounding a person in order and in line. Any spirit who wants to communicate with the living must first get the gatekeeper's go-ahead. When I do readings, I'll often clairvoyantly see a line of spirits waiting behind a closed door. Once I "open" myself up for business, it's the gatekeeper who comes through first, and this marks the start of the reading. Remember earlier when I compared the hundreds of excited spirits jumping up and down wanting to be heard at a group reading to a classroom of spirited preschoolers? It's my gatekeeper spirit who helps me keep this chaos under control, so that the spirits with the most urgent messages are heard first. My gatekeeper also protects me from any unwanted negative spiritual energy that may try to get in through the door. Gatekeepers are very loyal and protective. My gatekeeper looks not unlike singer-songwriter Pink—kind of edgy and punk. In the spiritual realm, my gatekeeper is a rock star, too, and I'm beyond grateful she's got my back.

PLACING THE CALL

Call on your gatekeeper, your permanent guides, and deceased loved ones to impress you with their insight in your waking hours and dream states. In addition, enlist the help of Archangel Metatron, whose name means "the throne beside the throne of God." You can't get much closer to God than that. Metatron is a big shot; he stands firmly in his truth and he can help you do the same. Say aloud, or just think: *Archangel Metatron, please help me to stand firmly in my truth and in my power, and to communicate in a way that reflects who and what I divinely am.*

reclaim: A RECAP

- The key to living a purposeful life lies in identifying how best you can embody God's divine love and light.

- In what direction do you feel divinely called? Don't think, *feel*. What does your intuitive wisdom tell you? Ask yourself, *What lights me up and makes me feel alive?*

- When you indentify and embrace your unique radiance, and when you use your special gifts and talents with the pure intention of serving others and spreading love, you're fulfilling your purpose—what you were born in this life to do.

- In the ancient Kabbalah tradition, the expression of divine power is referred to as *yesod,* and its energy resides in the sacral center, at the base of your pelvis. When *yesod* energy is awakened and unblocked, expect to feel solid in the foundation of who you are. Expect to feel powerful and empowered!

- As you continue to release the energy in your sacral center and stand firmly in your truth, call on your gatekeeper, your permanent guides, and deceased loved ones to impress you with their insight in your waking hours and dream states. For a conduit of *yesod* energy, call on Archangel Metatron to empower you to act as a unique expression and extension of God by *just being you.*

RISE UP

Once you embrace your unique radiance, standing firmly in your truth, then you can rise up and *live* your truth by shining your light brightly on the people and world around you. This is what it means to be God-like—a chip off the old block—and it's exactly what you were created for. It's the very reason you're alive.

Take a moment and let this sink in.

Not sure it sunk? Your ultimate purpose, what you were born to do in this lifetime, is to serve God by embodying God. Simply put, when your day-to-day, big and small actions, interactions, and reactions are an expression of love, light, beauty, gratitude, generosity, and kindness, that's exactly what you're doing—you're *being* God. In turn, you're also serving God and serving humanity. If this sounds like big-deal stuff, it is, and it comes with big rewards. When you consciously choose to surrender yourself day after day to God, your life takes on greater significance and meaning. Suddenly, every aspect of your life, from your career to your relationships to what you do beyond the nine-to-five grind has direction and purpose. And isn't that what you've been searching for all along?

Set the intention to live your truth—that is, to "rise up" by simply being your radiant self and extending your innate love and light to others. The road to purposeful fulfillment, where Heaven meets Earth, is just up ahead.

EMBODYING GOD

As you know by now, a typical day for me begins with some light and informal meditation and prayer. Before putting my feet onto the floor or over my first cup of coffee, I spend—give or take—five minutes surrendering myself to God's will. I close my eyes, take a few deep and easy breaths, and imagine drawing God's magnificent energy into me. This is similar to the visualization practice I provided earlier of plugging into God, except here I imagine slipping on a sheer, bright white bodysuit that, once I zip up, begins to merge with me; eventually we become one. I visualize my entire body glowing with light and love, and then I ask that all of my thoughts, words, and actions throughout the day be inspired by this same light, love, beauty, and kindness. I ask God to help me surrender my pesky ego and to use me instead to inspire, support, uplift, and heal others. As I continue to pray, I imagine shining light and love on my day and everyone in it. I start by visualizing my family, friends, and colleagues in a circle around me. I shine love and light their way. Then I imagine a circle of faceless silhouettes gathered around me, representing everyone I'll interact with and bump into throughout my day. I shine my love and light on them also and say the following "Early Rise" prayer under my breath: *Dear God and Guides, thank you for this day and for being with me in every way. I welcome your guidance, inspiration, and support as I show up today to carry out your will. Help me to stay in alignment with you and with my purpose for being. I'm grateful for the abundance of blessings, miracles, joy, and love that fills and surrounds me now and all throughout my day.*

After five minutes of quiet prayer, I slug down the remainder of my coffee and head out to the gym. Some days—actually *most* days—I'm absolutely blown away by how when I plug in, or "slip on" God, life flows almost effortlessly and easily. Not only that, I feel amazingly energized. And no, it's not from the coffee! It's because I'm running off of the most powerful source of energy that exists. No joke, when I start my day off by consciously rising up to be of service to God and surrendering myself to be used by Spirit to help the living, I have endless get-up-and-go at the gym. At the office, I feel creative and inspired and my readings tend to be spot-on. Back at home in the evening, I feel relaxed and present with my family. When I slip on God's bodysuit and set the intention to live my truth—that is, to be a unique expression of God—I simply don't sweat the small stuff. I feel too good to feel bad, and in this almost giddy state, I can often go for ten to fourteen hours straight without hitting a wall. Rather, at the end of the day, I feel happy, joyful, and naturally high. Also I feel a sense of divine approval, as if God's giving me a pat on the back for a job well done.

Sounds pretty incredible, doesn't it?

Truly, it is. And here's the kicker for starting off my day in this way: My life tends to effortlessly and easily fall into place. Synchronicities, little miracles, and signs pop up everywhere I go, validating that I'm in the positive flow of life, creating that divine timing, unfolding, and order I've been talking about throughout the ten steps of your awakening.

A few Saturdays ago, as I was driving to the gym thinking about the large audience reading I had later that night in downtown Denver, a car with the license plate BLESSME pulled in front of me. I thought, *Thank you, guides, for this amazing validation that I'm being supported on my path as I show up to serve those in need of healing, comfort, and guidance.* I really interpreted this as a literal sign that Spirit was blessing me and my work. Then, as soon as I walked through the front doors of the gym, the song "How to Save a Life" by the Fray started to play. I laughed out loud. This happens to be my dad's song; it was released right around the time of his death, and the lyrics especially spoke to me. . . . "Where did I go wrong? . . . I would have stayed up with you all night had I known how to save a life." For many years after Dad's suicide, I blamed myself for not claircognizantly knowing that he was in big trouble. As a spiritual medium, I felt like I should've picked up on his intentions and been able to intervene and save him before he took his own life. So when I heard "How to Save a Life" that morning at the gym, I understood that it was Dad's way of letting me know he was present with me and would again be present with me that night, guiding me from the other side when I'd more than likely attempt to make connections for people who'd lost a loved one to suicide. I smiled and acknowledged his presence. "Hi, Dad," I said. "I know we have work to do tonight. Thanks for being with me." To top off a synchronistic day, at the reading that night I heard the song again! Only this time I clairaudiently heard it playing in my mind at the same time I was picking up on the energy of a spirit named Matthew who clairvoyantly showed me that he'd overdosed with prescription pain pills. He wanted his father, who was sitting in the audience, to know that he was in a better place, retaking the tests he'd failed to pass in life and healing on the other side. This message brought tremendous closure to his father's grief, indicated by the heartfelt tears that streamed down his face.

Slipping on God's bodysuit is awesome, but eventually it wears off, which is why I take the time every morning (remember, just five minutes does the trick) to slip God's love and light back on. Just as you can't work out one day a week and expect your body to hold its shape, embodying God requires a maintenance plan. It doesn't just happen. Day after day, it requires your intention and attention. You must consciously make the choice to embody God. Marianne Williamson, who teaches *A Course in Miracles,* said in an interview once, "If we wake up in the morning and read the paper, listen to TV or the radio news, and add to that caffeine, then we go off to work without bothering to have spent even five minutes in search of God's peace, then how can we be perplexed that we're close to feeling depressed by noon?" She makes an excellent point. We feel our best and shine our brightest when we're regularly empowered with and embodying God's energy, with the purpose of serving others.

To give you another personal example of what it means to embody God, I want to share with you an experience I had, this time on the Dr. Phil show. I was invited onto the talk show to conduct a group reading for nine strangers to "prove" my mediumship skills and validate for the TV viewing audience that communication between the living and the dead is not only possible, but a regular occurrence. I willingly and happily accepted the invitation. I know what I do is real, and since the opportunity fell right into my lap, I figured it was God's way of saying, *Go, girl. Turn some skeptics into believers.*

The first day of production, I was escorted into a small room on the studio lot where nine people were somberly waiting for me to connect them with deceased loved ones. The reading, producers told me, would be taped and shown at a later date to a live studio audience who would determine if my gift was real. *Bring it,* I thought. Let the cameras roll. As soon as they did, I closed my eyes, invited Spirit in, and did my thing. After I had read the room for nearly an hour and made many solid connections with Spirit, the mood of the room lightened considerably. When I was finished, several people stood up and asked if they could give me a hug for making "such profound and healing" connections. I later overheard a few people say that I was "way better than the medium who'd read the group just before." Huh? I had no idea who they were talking about, or that I'd been a follow-up act.

The next day was the live studio audience portion of the talk show, with Dr. Phil as the host. I sat on stage with three colleagues who do spiritual work: Dougall Fraser, Colette Baron-Reid, and Glynis McCants, along with a staged psychic, named "Skeptic Jim." It was revealed to the rest of us on stage and the audience that he'd pretended to be a medium to demonstrate cold readings, a series of guessing techniques used by some mentalists, psychics, and fortune-tellers to determine details about another person, often in an effort to convince the person that the psychic knows something he or she actually doesn't. Cold readings can be convincing, but they're manipulative. They take advantage of people's grief, desperation, and emotional need for clarity and truth. It turned out that Skeptic Jim had used his cold reading skills on the same nine people I'd read the day before. So it was a setup, and now Dr. Phil was posing the following question to the studio audience: Who was more accurate? How do Jim and Rebecca compare?

Well, when they played back both Jim's and my taped readings from the day before, it was clear that where I provided very specific and heartfelt messages from Spirit that I could never have guessed, Jim was vague and cold. And when the nine participants were candidly asked how we compared with each other, nearly all of them said they could "feel" that something was off and wrong with Skeptic Jim the entire time. On the other hand they said that not long after I walked into the room, they felt that I was genuine. Can you guess why? Because I was *living my truth*—expressing and extending God's love and light in selfless service to other people in my own unique and special way. Not only do you feel your best and shine your brightest when you're embodying God, but also other people feel it, too. Divine radiance is felt.

When you started your own process of awakening in the beginning pages of this book, I explained that until you took the time to reflect and go within and remember who and what you are, the external pieces of your life wouldn't significantly shift or change. Well, that time has finally arrived, and now so long as you set the intention every day to rise up and live your truth, you'll be blessed with God's favor—meaning, as a fortune cookie once said to me, which I'll never forget: When you take care of God's work, God takes care of yours. Meaning, when you act with the pure intention to embody God's love and light, you set the tone for the rest of your life. Eventually, day by day and over time, every aspect of your life, from your relationships to your career, finances, and health and wellness, will effortlessly and easily fall into place. Embodying God puts you in the divine flow of life.

This popular fable sums it up well. Day after day a man prayed, "Dear God, help me to win the lottery." After months and months of this ritual, day after day, he finally heard a thunderous voice from the sky, "This is God speaking. In answer to your plea—yes, I will grant you your request to win the lottery, but will you do just *one* thing for me, please?"

"Yes, God, anything. You name it."

"Will you *please* go buy a ticket?"

God won't do for us what we can do for ourselves, so rise up and live your truth and then let God take care of the rest.

Still not entirely convinced?

Okay, let me give you a more tangible example. Are you familiar with the popular book and movie *The Pursuit of Happyness* by and about Chris Gardner? His is one of my all-time favorite stories and it's a perfect example of "rising up." This is the story of a man with an entrepreneurial spirit who invests his family's savings in a medical device he pitches to doctors. When no one bites and the investment fails, his family suffers financial ruin. Emotionally and economically stressed, his wife leaves him and their young son to make ends meet in San Francisco. After being evicted for unpaid income taxes, Gardner and his son are forced out on the street. At a very low point, Gardner and his son sleep overnight in public bathrooms. After many desperate months of hustling and nearly starving, they're taken in at a homeless shelter. On the verge of defeat, on the street one day Gardner synchronistically meets a manager from the stock brokerage firm Dean Witter, who is impressed by Gardner's charisma, raw ambition, and natural way with numbers—in other words, his divine radiance. On a whim, the manager gives Gardner his business card, and Gardner, who has nothing to lose, pursues the lead. He applies for a position at Dean Witter, and despite his past professional failures, his lack of an MBA or even a college degree, the firm decides to take a chance on him, offering him an unpaid position as an intern stockbroker. Gardner works like a dog, with a "no room for failure" mentality, in an effort to prove his worth and provide security, safety, and a future for his son. At the conclusion of his internship, he's offered a paid position. Gardner goes on to form his own multimillion-dollar brokerage firm, and today, in addition to running his successful business, he tours the country as a bestselling author giving motivational speeches about how to create a fulfilling, successful life. Success, he explains, is not about money. For Gardner, success came after months and months of rising up every day to do and *be* his best for his son in the one way he knew how—by combining his natural talent with numbers and his entrepreneurial spirit in service to others. Today, Gardner is involved with homelessness initiatives assisting families to stay intact. He serves on the board of the International Rescue Committee, and he's helped fund a project that creates low-income housing and employment opportunities in one of San Francisco's poorest neighborhoods. Gardner's continuing success is a reflection of the choices he makes day-to-day to rise up and embody God's love, light, generosity, and kindness.

Gardner's story is amazing and his impact is impressive, and while his life may look very different from your own—obviously, not everyone is destined to be a high-powered stockbroker, and thankfully, not everyone will suffer homelessness—the principle of rising up is the same for you as it is for him. When you humbly show up every day with the pure intention to combine your divine radiance and unique talents with service to others, you'll be doing what you were born to do and "happyness" will be yours.

FINDING HAPPYNESS:

Justine's Story

It was Labor Day weekend and I was at work. I was sitting alone in the break room in my scrubs, and I began to reflect. While many of my friends and family had the day off, I realized that I wouldn't want to be anywhere else. I love my job. I'm an obstetrician, and on an average week, I deliver up to ten babies. I've been doing this for over fifteen years, so you do the math—that's a lot of kids.

So I'm sitting in the break room feeling so lucky and grateful for my job. I know a lot of people who hate their jobs, or don't even have jobs, and I get to do something every day that I consider to be both a joy and a privilege and which literally brings life into the world.

I sat in silent gratitude for about five minutes, saying, "Thank you, thank you, thank you," and that's when my beeper went off. I was being called to deliver, not one, but eight babies in a row that day! It's like God heard me bragging about my cool job and then said, "Okay, if you like it so much, here you go!"

After fourteen hours on my feet, I drove home and passed out. But when I woke up the next morning, I still felt lucky. I wouldn't have changed a thing, and in fact, I was ready to do it all over again.

AWAKEN RADIANCE

It takes tremendous courage, commitment, and discipline to rise up every day and live your truth, but this is what a purposeful life is all about. The following EnLighten Up meditation is designed to help you in this effort by unblocking the energy in your root center at the base of your spine. Root energy grounds you to the Earth, and when it's flowing freely within you, you'll feel grounded and centered, enabling you to take day-to-day deliberate, down-to-Earth actions that manifest a purposeful life. According to Dr. Hiroshi Motoyama, in *Theories of the Chakras*, when root energy is in the process of awakening, the area around the navel feels filled with energy and there can be a sensation of tremendous heat.

After working for fifteen years as an entertainment agent in Hollywood, Elisa realized one day she was called to do something else. Her wake-up call came on the heels of a personal crash. Her glamorous Hollywood lifestyle had fostered less than glamorous habits. She'd become an alcoholic and a drug addict, and in seeking treatment for herself, she realized that if she used her unique talent for motivating people, and for making important connections and relationships, in combination with service to those who similarly struggled with substance abuse, she'd be doing "work that I've come to see as the highest use of my talents at this point in my life." After fifteen years as a successful agent for TV and movie stars, she left the business and created a case management business for drug and alcohol dependents and opened a sober living home for young adult males. She wrote about her experi-

ENLIGHTEN UP:

Release Your Spine

Close your eyes and become aware of the rhythm of your breath. Let it slow down. As you slowly breathe in through your nose and exhale through your mouth, imagine yourself in your favorite natural setting. Visualize yourself as a magnificent tree, with your head reaching high into the sky and your feet rooted in the earth below.

Continue to breathe.

Now visualize a spark of ruby-red light at the base of your spine. Within the Tree of Life, this energy is rooted deep in the earth, at the farthest reaches of the root system. With each breath, feel this intense ruby-red light expand and brighten your root center. With each inhalation, imagine this ruby-red light expand, loosen, open, and release any stuck energy that's blocking the flow of light throughout your body and standing in the way of you rising up and living your truth.

Breathe deeply and easily.

Set the intention to rise up and shine, and to feel safe and secure in the world. Throughout the rest of your day, let your breath serve as a reminder that you're an extension of God, and as such, divine radiance resides within you. If you forget or doubt this, repeat mentally or out loud: *I am safe, secure, divinely protected, and guided at all times. I trust that the presence of God supports me to rise up into my greatness, being the highest and best version of me.*

ence in the *Daily Beast*, "Five years into my sobriety, I realized I was being called to serve it as it had served me. I got it on a visceral level that many people, who have slid down the same hellhole I fell down, don't have the inner or the outer resources to get out of it that I did. And thus, the change that I'm making now." This story perfectly illustrates what it means to rise up.

CALLING FOR BACKUP

To help you rise up and embody God, who better to call on than incarnated beings of light—other flesh-and-blood people just like you? Call on the people in your life whose energy helps ground and center you—friends, family members, and colleagues whose presence tends to calm and comfort you, whose words offer you clarity, and whose actions tend to inspire you to rise up and be the best version of yourself day-to-day.

I refer to these people as my "ground crew." When I'm not asking Spirit for advice, guidance, strength, and faith, I'm hitting up my best and brightest peeps on the ground. While I'm blessed to have several close friends, my best friend Katie is my number one go-to when things get tough and rising up feels like the last thing I want to do. Whatever roadblock gets in my way, I know I can call her and she'll say, "Time-out," and then proceed to remind me of my greatness, my potential, my divine radiance. Sometimes, she'll call me out of the blue and say, "I just had a weird dream about you. What's up?" As I often say, you can run but you can't hide from Spirit. Our energy

INCARNATED BEINGS OF LIGHT

These are living, breathing people who seem wise and enlightened beyond their years. Most of us know people like this, commonly referred to as old souls or advanced souls, whose energy tends to both calm and uplift us and whose actions inspire us to reach our highest potential and purpose. Typically, these "light workers" are children and adults who have lived before, and whether they realize it or not (most don't), they've left the spirit world to return again to the physical world with the gift of clear insight and higher knowledge, to help and heal the people they come into contact with.

holds our thoughts and feelings, which we're telepathically sending out at all times. So my guides know all too well when I need help and I'm just too proud or stubborn to ask for it. They intervene when I've withdrawn by gently nudging Katie in her sleep, inspiring her to reach out and support me.

Who's in your ground crew? Take an inventory of who these people are and allow them to help you. Little known fact: Most people like to be asked for help. This provides them with an occasion to show up, step up, and rise up on their own by extending love and light your way. Everybody benefits.

GROUND CREW

Sometimes you need look no farther than the actual ground for your ground crew. Our pets, especially our dogs and cats, are not only great companions, but also serve to inspire us to rise up. They teach us patience, encourage us to play and be present, help us heal in difficult times, and often inspire us to extend loving-kindness in the same selfless way they extend it to us. Because their energy is so pure, positive, and aligned with God, just being around our pets has the potential to shift our energy up.

PLACING THE CALL

In addition to calling on your ground crew, ask the angelic realm to inspire you. Call on Archangel Sandalphon, who helps us to rise up and fulfill our purpose. Archangel Sandalphon is often depicted as one of the tallest angels, so that he may easily reach Heaven from Earth, and in meditation he has clairvoyantly appeared to me as a gentle giant wearing trousers and a button-down shirt. What can I say—he looks like a down-to-Earth kinda guy, and as a representative of the lowest order of angels assisting humanity directly, he helps us to stay grounded and focused on who we are and what we're meant to do in our lifetimes.

Say aloud, or just think: *Archangel Sandalphon, deliverer and answerer of all prayers, please take my sacred requests to the realm of Spirit, placing them in the hands of God. Help me to ground my spirit into physical reality, to ground Heaven into Earth, and to make my life a living prayer. Teach me how to use my God-given talents to make the world a better place. Thank you. Amen.*

rise up: A RECAP

· Your true purpose, what you were born to do in this lifetime, is to serve God by embodying God. Simply put, when your day-to-day, big and small actions, interactions, and reactions are an expression of love, light, beauty, gratitude, generosity, and kindness, that's exactly what you're doing.

· Just as you can't work out one day a week and expect your body to hold its shape, embodying God requires a maintenance plan. Day after day, it requires your intention and attention. You must consciously make the choice to embody God.

· When you act with the pure intention to serve as a unique expression and energetic extension of divine love and light, you set the tone for the rest of your life. Eventually, day by day and over time, every aspect of your life, from your relationships to your career, finances, and health and wellness, will divinely flow.

· In the ancient Kabbalah tradition, the expression and *manifestation* of your divine radiance in the physical form is called *malchut,* and its energy resides at the base of your spine. When *malchut* energy is awakened—when your words, actions, and deeds are the embodiment of God—expect to feel radiant! Expect to feel an energetic shift where the spiritual and physical worlds converge to create your kingdom—Heaven on Earth.

· In addition to calling on your ground crew, ask the angelic realm to help you rise up. For a conduit of *malchut* energy, call on Archangel Sandalphon to help you stay grounded and focused on embodying God day to day.

PART THREE

REACH HIGHER

—◄o►—

ACCORDING TO THE ancient Kabbalah tradition, it's the fate of man to descend from the higher spiritual realm into the physical everyday world to learn who he (or she) really is—a unique expression and divine extension of God. Once we become grounded in the knowing of who and what we truly are and from where we came, we can begin to fulfill our purpose by rising up and embodying our divinity while still in a physical body. And when we do, almost as soon as we begin to *be God,* we begin the ascent back home. This doesn't mean you leave your body; you still remain grounded in the physical world, but you *feel* different. You begin to experience a lightness, a brightness, a sense of finally being *free*. When you act as an expression and extension of God's love and light, don't be surprised to feel your energetic body begin to buzz, vibrate, and rise to a higher level, where you experience the blissful sensation of soaring in your everyday waking life. This is what it means to be a "free spirit." In Sanskrit, this spiritual metamorphosis is referred to as *muladhara* and is associated with new beginnings. I call it being awake.

And so now that you are wide awake—what next?

It's simple, really. As you move forward with your life, set the intention day to day to live in an awakened state. Whatever life situations you find yourself in—take a moment to step back through the awakening process. Go inward. Quiet your mind. Put faith and trust in your divine wisdom and guidance. Accept responsibility and hold yourself accountable for your choices. Face life's challenges head-on, with the intent to learn from them. Release your fears. Extend loving-kindness. Be grateful. Let go of the desire to control outcomes. Rest assured that your life is unfolding just as it's meant to, and then just be your unique and radiant self. When you approach life every day in this intentional and purposeful way, an abundance of happiness, harmony, and spiritual fulfillment is yours today, tomorrow, and until the final moments of your life.

For nearly fifteen years now, I've communicated with spirits who desperately and passionately want to help the living wake up. They want their living loved ones to remember who and what they are, and what they came here to do. What Spirit confirms for me on a daily basis is that how you approach and live your life has enduring effects. The choices you make, along with the intentions behind your actions, reactions, and interactions, can either stall your spiritual growth or advance it. In my meditations, dreams, and readings, what Spirit has impressed upon me time and time again, on a clairvoyant, clairaudient, claircognizant, and clairsentient level, is that there is a life review process once our body dies a physical death and our spirit leaves the Earth plane and makes the ascent back home, in which we carefully reflect upon and review our life and determine how well we fulfilled our purpose. We sit as judge and jury along with our deceased loved ones, angels, and guides, and honestly assess how well we passed our own tests. As we were challenged along the road of life, how well did we do? In what ways did we succeed, and in what ways did we fail? Spirits consistently relay the message that when we die, we ascend to the level we've "earned" based on our willingness and efforts to *be God.* Recognizing both our strengths and shortcomings, in what ways can we do better, reach higher, the next go-round? While we firmly hold ourselves accountable for our choices, Spirit has impressed upon me that the life review process is a gentle, reflective one where we take a truthful look in the mirror and accept ourselves and our lives for what they were and subsequently plan for what comes next. Together with our Team Spirit, we draft the contract for our next life, setting into motion specific events and circumstances to show up as opportunities to further learn and master the lessons that will best help promote our spiritual growth. Once our spirit is rested and restored, many of us will slip back into a human body and buy another ticket for the roller-coaster ride of life.

Another ticket?

Don't freak. Understand that no one's going to get it perfectly right the first time around. Remember, it takes most of us many lifetimes before we start to get it *at all.* And anyway, perfection is not the point or the goal. There's a popular Buddhist teaching that it's not what we achieve in our lives but what we die trying to achieve that gives meaning to our existence. Spirit has similarly communicated to me that it is our pure intention, daily devotion, and sincere willingness to learn, grow, and become lighter, brighter, and closer to God that gives our lives purpose and meaning. That said, daily devotion to living a purposeful life takes work, the hardest assignment being to remember day to day that you are indeed divine. With that knowing and that memory comes the responsibility to act *as if*, and acting as an extension of God often requires that we make adjustments and changes, both significant and incremental, to our lives. Change like this can feel scary, overwhelming, and sometimes even threatening, but so long as you make the conscious choice today and every day to rise up and express the love and light within you, shining your unique and divine radiance into the dark corners of the world, there's nothing to fear.

OH WOW

From all the accounts I've read, I'm pretty convinced that in his final moments, Steve Jobs, the American entrepreneur best known as the cofounder, chairman, and chief executive officer of Apple Inc., understood what I'm telling you now. In his autobiography, Jobs openly writes that despite his professional success and popularity, he made some bad personal choices, often acting selfishly—in effect, not rising up for his children, his friends, and his wife. Yet at the end, he emphatically wanted his loved ones at his bedside. Just before slipping into unconsciousness, he looked past his sister, children, and wife and said, "Oh wow. Oh wow. Oh wow."

My brother Rabbi Baruch HaLevi incorporated Steve Jobs's final words into his 2012 Rosh Hashanah sermon, and I couldn't have said it better myself. "As Jobs lay in his bed dying, his final words were not spent talking about the upcoming iPhone 5 or the newest version of the iPad. Rather, Steve's final moments were spent talking with his family, and clearly touching upon something transcendent, beautiful, and awesome as he departed this world with the final words 'Oh wow! Oh wow! Oh wow!' upon his breath.

"We shouldn't have to wait until we die to wake up and be amazed at what this world has to offer. We need not wait to have an awesome glimpse into the mystery as we transition into death. The Days of Wow are here, giving us plenty of opportunities to stop what we are doing, to take stock of how we are living, to pay attention to everyone and everything all around us and say 'Oh Wow! Oh Wow! Oh Wow!' time and time again."

AWAKEN THE SPIRIT WITHIN

Your Day of Wow is here. This final EnLighten Up meditation unifies all ten steps of the awakening process by lighting up your spiritual and energetic body one divine expression at a time, from the tips of your toes up through the crown of your head, so that God's powerful energy and divine radiance can flow freely through you, *as you*. It's

ENLIGHTEN UP:

Lighting The Tree of Life

Begin by sitting in a comfortable position, with your spine straight and body centered. Spend the next two to three minutes breathing slowly and deeply, quieting your mind and relaxing your body.

Once you feel calm, clear, and focused, bring your attention to the base of your spine. Imagine that with each breath, you're stretching roots deep down into the earth. Feel them sink down into the dark soil. With each breath, allow this root system to go even deeper, creating a solid anchor that grounds and centers you in your body and in this world. Pause and silently give thanks for your physical body that allows you to travel down the roadways of life.

With your next breath, visualize a ruby-red spark of light rising up through the earth. Begin drawing this energy into your body at the base of your spine. With each breath, feel this intense ruby-red light expand and brighten, awakening *malchut*, the expression of divine radiance, within you, where the spiritual and physical worlds converge to create your kingdom—Heaven on Earth. Set the intention to rise up, embody God, and act in service to humankind. Call on Archangel Sandalphon and your ground crew to help you in your ongoing effort to live your life on purpose.

Continue to breath.

Feel this surge of energy travel up your body into your sacral center, the space in between your hips. This energy gives off the color of amber-orange light. Allow this energy to expand and brighten, awakening *yesod,* your divine truth. Set the intention to reclaim your power and unique radiance. Call on Archangel Metatron, your gatekeeper, and your permanent spirit guides to help empower you.

Continue to breathe.

With your next breath, imagine this amber-orange light growing brighter and brighter, awakening now *hod,* the divine light of surrender and acceptance, within you. Set the intention to surrender control and resistance and accept the things you cannot change. Call on Archangel Raziel and your visiting guides to help you let go and let God.

Continue to breathe.

With your next deep breath in, feel the spark of *netzach* grow brighter within you, awakening divine victory, faith, and trust. Set the intention to free your conscious and unconscious mind of any fears, skepticism, or doubt. Call on Archangel Uriel and your visiting spirit guides to help you feel assured that your life is unfolding according to plan.

Now shift gears and concentrate on pulling God's energy up into your belly. With each inhalation, imagine a golden-yellow light filling up every inch of your solar plexus, awakening *tiferet,* the divine light of gratitude and beauty within you. Set the intention to feel a depth of appreciation for everything and everyone in your life. Call on Archangel Raphael and your council of guides to help you see the gift in every situation in your life.

Next, breathe deeply in and out and draw divine energetic light up into your heart. It will turn a brilliant emerald green. Feel your heart open and soften with each healing breath, awakening *gevurah*, divine strength, within you. Set the intention to release your fears and create healthy boundaries when necessary. Call on Archangel Gabriel and the Ascended Masters for protection and guidance.

Continue to focus on your heart center and take another deep inhale, awakening *chesed*, divine loving-kindness, within you. With each breath, set the intention to freely and easily feel, be, and extend love to the world around you. Call on Archangel Michael and the Ascended Masters to help you *be love*.

Breathe deeply and easily.

Now allow this growing flow of divine energy to come up into your throat, where it turns the color of sky blue. Feel it expand and loosen your throat, awakening *da'at*, deep realization and divine knowing, within you. As you breathe into the pool of energy at your throat, set the intention to have an aha moment in which you recognize the role you're playing in every event, situation, and circumstance that shows up in your life.

Next, feel the energy rise into your inner eye, the space just above your eyebrows, in the center of your forehead. The light that this energy emanates is indigo blue. With each breath, allow this intense indigo light to grow brighter and brighter, awakening *binah*, divine understanding, within you. Set the intention to understand the life lessons being presented to you. Call on Archangel Jophiel and your guardian angels for help in seeing your life through God's eyes.

Continue to breathe.

Take another deep inhale and awaken *chokmah*, your

divine wisdom and intuition. Set the intention now to see what you need to see in this moment to guide you forward on your path. Call on Archangel Peliel to help you trust and act on your intuitive guidance.

Continue to breathe.

Feel the energy in your mind's eye travel upward and above your head where it illuminates your "crown," creating a glow of violet-white light. With each breath in and out, allow this violet light to grow more and more radiant, awakening *keter*, divine knowing, within you. As you continue to breathe deeply and easily, set the intention to open yourself up and be a clear channel for God's powerful love and light. Call on Archangel Akatriel and all of divinity to remind you of who and what you are, a unique and radiant expression of God.

Sit for a few more minutes and visualize yourself as a magnificent tree, your feet rooted deep in the earth and your arms stretching outward and reaching high into the sky above. Take one final deep breath and *rise up*. And as you do, feel your energetic and spiritual body awaken, receiving and radiating a single bright, brilliant, and powerful light—the light of God, residing within you and around you—as you.

been inspired by countless validations from spirits who have clairvoyantly shown me the Tree of Life as a metaphor for spiritual awakening. Only after descending from the spiritual realm into the dense physical world of *Malchut* can we rise up, ascend the Tree of Life, and make the journey back home.

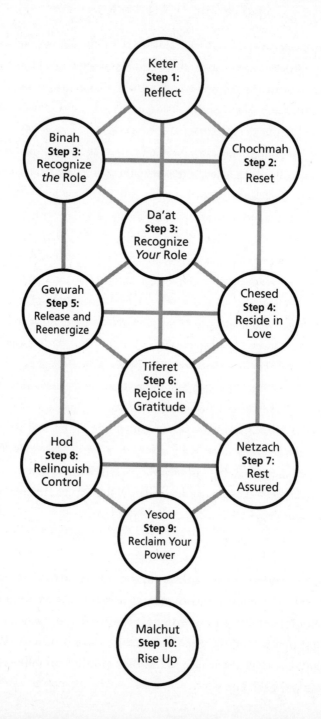

A month ago I had a visitation from my father, Shelly. He "called" me in my dream. I was standing on the front porch of the house I grew up in, and he called me on my cell phone. I could hear his voice clear as day, just as if he were on the other end of the line. Connecting with him woke me up in my dream, meaning that I became conscious although I remained asleep. Not wanting to lose our connection, I kept my eyes shut and we had ninety powerful seconds together before the line became static and he cut out.

Understand that a spiritual visitation is different from feeling a spirit's presence. I feel and sense my dad's presence all the time in readings and in meditation. He subtly impresses me with words, thoughts, and visions, but a visitation is as real and solid as talking to someone in real life. As far as I'm concerned—it *is* real!

I'd been praying for Dad to visit me since the publication of my first book, *Spirited,* and so when he showed up in my dream, I started crying tears of joy. He agreed it was an incredible and priceless moment we were sharing together. Once his energy began to pull back and disappear, I opened my eyes and looked at the clock. It was 1:42 A.M. I scribbled down the time in a notepad on my bedside table so I wouldn't forget, and then I played back our visit in my mind. In the dream, Dad referenced a specific situation I was struggling with, and he wanted me to know he understood well my personal challenges and intended life lessons. While he couldn't tell me what to do (that's up to me and my free will), he was guiding me as best he could from the other side. He did impart that no matter how I decided to resolve the situation, to remember that life is meant to be joyful and beautiful—*heavenly*. I thought it was a little odd that Dad hadn't signed off with one of his favorite sayings: "Everything's going to be okay," but I quickly dismissed it because the messages he did pass on within that short amount of time were so reassuring and profound, leaving me with a renewed sense of awe for how the unseen world watches, guides, and comforts us.

Later that morning, once I'd had a chance to truly wake up, the number 142 popped back into my mind. I was reminded of the time on the clock after my visit with Dad had ended. On a whim, I looked up the significance of the number 142 according to Doreen Virtue, a trusted colleague and the author of *Angel Numbers*. Based on her research and divine insights, 142 means: The angels want you to know that *everything's okay*. I laughed out loud. So typical! Even in spirit, Dad's always getting the last word.

While I connect deceased loved ones with their living loved ones every day, I'm not often on the receiving end myself. Experiencing a long-awaited visitation from my father while finishing up this book was so important for me, to re-remember how powerful it is to not only believe, but also know that we are never separate and alone. Rather, we are all in this together. We are all here on this earth plane, in this exact moment in time, to learn, to grow, and to remember who and what we truly are. And we've each made the choice to be here for this express purpose.

Before you began the process of awakening, I asked you, "What would it be like to feel, to experience the knowing that we are all energetic extensions of God's love and light? Would it change how you felt about yourself and your life? Would it change how you felt about other people?"

While you quietly answer that question for yourself, I'll tell you that knowing what I know now, I absolutely feel differently. One of the most significant changes I've experienced over the years is a shift in perception, where I no longer see myself as separate from the world around me. In fact, I no longer see my life as that much different from my clients' or my neighbor across the street. While a client of mine may have suffered the loss of a child in this lifetime and I haven't, I've recently suffered the death of a marriage. Both are painful, encompassing similar feelings of grief and loss, and both are equally significant lessons and opportunities for spiritual growth. So while someone else's life may look very different from yours, understand that we are all on the same road. We may be driving at varying speeds, choosing different lanes, and taking alternate exits, but we're ultimately trying to get to the same place—closer to our truth and closer to God. We're just going about getting there in our own individual way. Understanding this, who are we to judge where on the road of life anyone is?

Lately, I've been imagining what it might be like if people took a more curious and compassionate versus competitive approach with one another. Specifically, what if we stopped asking each other, "What do you *do*?" and instead wondered aloud, "What lessons are you here to learn, and how's that going so far?" In this imaginary scenario, there'd no doubt be a few—*huh?*—perplexed and defeated reactions. To these individuals, I might say, "If you're not sure, or if you don't *remember,* I know a few people to call to help jog your memory."

The unseen world—our guides and angels and deceased loved ones—are present with us every day, waiting for us to call on them to lovingly guide us along, and nudge us to wake up to *who we truly are and what we're meant to do.* As above so below, in Spirit and on Earth, we're all connected to and interconnected with each other by a single bright, brilliant, and powerful light—the unconditional love of God. In this life and the next, expressing and extending your "God-spark" is all you're meant to do. My sincere and deep hope is that you now remember this fundamental truth, too.

Appendix

Step 1: ARCHANGEL AKATRIEL

As a conduit of crown energy (divine knowing), Archangel Akatriel is the guy to call to awaken your knowing that God is within you, as you. Akatriel is considered to be the most powerful and supreme of all the archangels. His name means the "crown of the source of the whole of existence." He's referred to as the link between God and humanity. In other words: He's the closest thing to God's powerful energy. Archangel Akatriel specifically gives us the gift of clear thought, which helps open our minds to seeing beyond who and what we think we are and knowing on a deep soul level that we're energetic extensions of God.

To call on Archangel Akatriel, just think or say aloud: *Archangel Akatriel, please be with me. Please help me to remember my divine radiance and help me to feel connected to God, the source of my divinity.*

Step 2: ARCHANGEL PELIEL

On days when you're feeling lost, directionless, or even just the slightest bit foggy, specifically call on Archangel Peliel, whose name means the "wonderment of God," to give you guidance. Because he's a conduit of *chokmah* energy (divine guidance), ask Archangel Peliel to help you see your life more clearly and find the answers you've been searching for.

To call on Archangel Peliel, just think or say aloud: *Archangel Peliel, please be with me. Please help me to see clearly. I'm calling on you now to help me reset my divine wisdom, my intuitive guidance. Help me to trust and follow my intuition to guide me forward in big and small ways.*

Step 3: ARCHANGEL JOPHIEL

As a conduit of *binah* energy (divine understanding), Archangel Jophiel can be called on to specifically help you recognize the life lessons being presented to you and realize the role you're playing in your day-to-day life. Archangel Jophiel is often referred to as both the "Beauty of God," and "Divine Beauty," and in addition to inspiring you with beautiful thoughts, Jophiel can also help you recognize the lessons that have purposefully, and often quite beautifully, shown up in your life.

To call on Archangel Jophiel, just think or say aloud: *Archangel Jophiel, please be with me. Please fill my heart with forgiveness and help me to see clearly. Please help me see through God's eyes and make choices that will positively benefit everyone involved.*

Step 4: ARCHANGEL MICHAEL

As a conduit of *chesed* energy (divine loving-kindness), Archangel Michael can be called on to specifically help you heal and open your heart so that you can freely and easily feel, be, and extend love to the world around you. Archangel Michael, whose name in Hebrew literally means "who is like God," is the messenger of love, mercy, generosity, and kindness. In addition to helping awaken loving kindness within you, he's a great protector. Call on him to give you courage in times of fear.

To call on Archangel Michael, just think or say aloud: *Archangel Michael, please be with me. Please help to protect me and remind me of my divine loving nature. Inspire me to make day-to-day decisions and take actions based in love, compassion, and kindness.*

Step 5: ARCHANGEL GABRIEL

To help you release your fears and create healthy boundaries, specifically call on Archangel Gabriel, known as the messenger angel and the "strength of God." As a conduit of *gevurah* energy (divine strength), Archangel Gabriel will step in and do battle on your behalf against external energy that does not serve you and that you feel unable to conquer.

To call on Archangel Gabriel, just think or say aloud: *Archangel Gabriel, thank you for helping me to conquer any fear or opposing forces that may stand in my way. I welcome your strength and protection. Thank you for fully shielding me today from all darkness, negativity, and fear I may encounter. Please bounce all negativity off and away from me. Let my light transform all darkness back into love.*

Step 6: ARCHANGEL RAPHAEL

On days when you're struggling to feel gratitude or recognize the beauty in a person, situation, or circumstance in your life, specifically call on Archangel Raphael, known as the "Physician of God" and "God Heals." As a conduit of *tiferet* energy (divine gratitude) he provides physical and emotional healing by helping you see the gift in every situation in your life.

To call on Archangel Raphael, just think or say aloud: *Archangel Raphael, thank you for being with me now, and for your help in opening my heart to freely give and receive love. May this opening serve to awaken gratitude within me, allowing me to fully appreciate and see the beauty in everything and everyone that shows up in my life.*

Step 7: ARCHANGEL URIEL

On days when you're struggling with skepticism, fear, or doubt, call on Archangel Uriel, known as the "Light of God," to heighten your trust as you tackle and try to resolve each of life's challenges. A conduit of *netzach* energy (divine faith and trust), the presence of Archangel Uriel will assure you that your life is unfolding according to plan.

To call on Archangel Uriel, just think or say aloud: *Archangel Uriel, thank you for filling me with the divine trust of God, thereby relieving me of all self-doubt and fear. May your presence light the way in helping me to resolve any challenges I might face, restoring order and faith in my life.*

Step 8: ARCHANGEL RAZIEL

If you haven't yet realized what the challenges in your life are trying to teach you, then specifically ask Archangel Raziel, known as the "prince of knowledge of hidden things" to help you relinquish control and give you faith and trust that your life is unfolding just as it's meant to. Because he is a conduit of *hod* energy (divine surrender and acceptance), ask Archangel

Raziel to help you surrender your fears and doubts and accept the things you cannot change.

To call on Archangel Raziel, just think or say aloud: *Archangel Raziel, please help me to let go of any limiting beliefs, doubts, worries, and fears that may be keeping me blocked or stuck. Thank you for filling me with assurance that everything in my life is unfolding according to divine timing, and for guiding me along and validating for me that I'm on the right path.*

Step 9: ARCHANGEL METATRON

To assist you in consciously showing up every day to do the job you were born to do—act as a unique expression and extension of God by *just being* you—specifically call on Archangel Metatron, whose name means the "throne beside the throne of God." Because he is a conduit of *yesod* energy (divine truth), call on Archangel Metatron to help you reclaim your power by expressing and extending your unique radiance to the world around you.

To call on Archangel Metatron, just think or say aloud: *Archangel Metatron, please help me to stand firmly in my truth and in my power, and to communicate in a way that reflects who and what I divinely am.*

Step 10: ARCHANGEL SANDALPHON

To help you rise up, embody God, and act in service to humankind, specifically call on Archangel Sandalphon, often depicted as one of the tallest angels so that he may easily reach Heaven from Earth. As a conduit of *malchut* energy (where the spiritual and physical worlds converge), Archangel Sandalphon will help you stay grounded and focused on your effort to live your life on purpose.

To call on Archangel Sandalphon, just think or say aloud: *Archangel Sandalphon, help me to ground my spirit into physical reality, to ground Heaven into Earth, and to make my life a living prayer. Teach me how to use my God-given talents to make the world a better place.*

Acknowledgments

Once again I am deeply humbled to have the opportunity to write a book that imparts the wisdom and insights of Spirit. While it has been a tremendous undertaking, it's been an invaluable experience and one which I could not have had if it weren't for my "Team Spirit," both in Heaven and on Earth.

First and foremost, words fail to express how fortunate I feel to have had the creative efforts and assistance of my brilliantly talented cowriter, Samantha Rose. I'm deeply thankful for her ongoing dedication and priceless contribution to this project, which gave it a life of its own.

My sincere appreciation to Yfat Reiss Gendell, literary agent and dear friend, who has taken me under her wing since our partnership began five years ago. Her calm, cool, and collected presence, along with her rock-solid faith in the process, have served to raise me up to my highest potential. I'm blessed to work with her and the entire Foundry team, especially Stephanie Abou, whose ongoing hard work and support in getting my books into the foreign markets has surpassed my expectations.

This book would not be what it is if it had not been for the vision and guiding light of my God-sent editor, Gary Jansen. Gary provided me with his support both as an editor and as a vast resource of information and wisdom. His genius insights and direction resulted in me digging deeper in an effort to create a book reflecting my highest truth. His editorial assistance was beyond invaluable, and I hope the final product is worthy of his confidence and faith.

To the wonderful team at Crown, I thank them all for their enthusiasm, support, and faith in the evolution of this book. I consider myself extremely fortunate to be in their hands and extend my heartfelt appreciation for their belief in my message and me.

Dr. David Sanders has been my Kabbalah teacher and friend, whose knowledge and guidance have been invaluable and greatly appreciated. When I needed his assistance in combining my information with the Jewish Kabbalah, he was there to impart his wisdom and knowledge each step of the way. His examples of a relentless search for truth and of living his truth have been both inspiring and fundamental in my spiritual growth.

The journey of doing the work and growing my gift awakened the best in me, which would not have been possible without the personal and professional support and love over the years of Brian Rosen. Deep and sincere thanks to him for assisting me in reaching those in need.

For my two greatest teachers and blessings in this lifetime, Jakob and Sam, who continuously share their love and light by simply being themselves, I am forever thankful.

Thanks to my mom, for everything she is and has been and always will be for me . . . serving as one of my greatest earth angels. And to my step-dad, Howard, for his loving support, assistance, and guidance on every level, I am truly grateful.

Thanks to my Grandma Flo, for always being one of my biggest cheerleaders and positive role models along my path.

To my adored brothers, Baruch and Zach, and my sister-in-law, Ariela, whose own journeys of awakening and evolving continue to be a source of inspiration.

My special energy healer and friend, Ariel Hardy, divinely came into my life seven years ago and has since served to keep me grounded and humble, while at the same time expanding my gift and allowing my spirit to soar. I'm incredibly appreciative of her presence in my life, along with her willingness to serve as a pillar of light and healing for so many.

Thanks also to the rest of my family and my many special friends and spiritual companions—old and new—for blessing my life with rich friendship, joy, and love. Each person contributes in his or her own unique way to my awakening, continuous unfolding, and becoming more of who I am. I am blessed to have such a solid "ground crew" (happy Buddha included) supporting, protecting, inspiring, and loving me along the way. May they all someday know just how much they've touched my life.

My deepest thanks goes out to all my clients who shared their stories in this book. It is my hope that through their experiences and growth, others will be comforted and inspired. In addition, I don't take for granted my loyal clientele that allows me the ongoing opportunity to share my gift and fulfill my purpose every day.

Of my guides, MC and M3, and my dad, whose silent

partnership in spirit has served as my strength, courage, and guiding light each step of the way, I'm in constant awe and appreciation.

To all of the above, deep and heartfelt thanks and all love, as I would not be where I am without you and your presence along my journey. *Namaste.*